Jaguar XKE Collection No.1

Compiled by
R.M. Clarke

ISBN 0 907 073 085

**Distributed by
Brooklands Book Distribution,
'Holmerise', Seven Hills Road,
Cobham, Surrey, England.**

Brooklands Books Titles in this series

AC Cobra 1962-1969
Armstrong Siddeley Cars 1945-1960
Austin 7 in the 30's
Austin Seven Cars 1930-1935
Austin 10 1932-1939
Austin Healey 100 1952-1959
Austin Healey 3000 1959-1967
Bentley Cars 1919-1929
Bentley Cars 1929-1934
Bentley Cars 1934-1939
Bentley Cars 1940-1945
Bentley Cars 1945-1950
BMW 1600 Collection No. 1
BMW 2002 Collection No. 1
Buick Cars 1929-1939
Camaro 1966-1970
Chrysler Cars 1930-1939
Citroen Traction Avant 1934-1957
Corvette Cars 1955-1964
Datsun 240z & 260z 1970-1977
De Tomaso Collection No. 1
Dodge Cars 1924-1938
Ferrari Cars 1946-1956
Ferrari Cars 1957-1962
Ferrari Cars 1962-1966
Ferrari Cars 1966-1969
Ferrari Cars 1969-1973
Ferrari Cars 1973-1977
Ferrari Cars 1977-1981
Ferrari Collection No. 1
Fiat X1/9 1972-1980
Ford GT 40 1964-1978
Ford Mustang 1964-1967
Ford Mustang 1967-1973
Hudson & Railton Cars 1936-1940
Jaguar (& S.S) Cars 1931-1937
Jaguar (& S.S) Cars 1937-1947
Jaguar Cars 1948-1951
Jaguar Cars 1951-1953
Jaguar Cars 1954-1955
Jaguar Cars 1955-1957
Jaguar Cars 1957-1961
Jaguar Cars 1961-1964
Jaguar Cars 1964-1968
Jaguar Sports Cars 1957-1960
Jaguar E-Type 1961-1966
Jaguar E-Type 1966-1971
Jaguar E-Type 1971-1975
Jaguar XKE Collection No. 1
Jaguar XJ6 1968-1972
Jaguar XJ6 1973-1980
Jaguar XJ12 1972-1980
Jaguar XJS 1975-1980
Jensen Cars 1946-1967
Jensen Cars 1967-1979
Jensen Interceptor 1966-1976
Jensen-Healey 1972-1976
Lamborghini Cars 1964-1970
Lamborghini Cars 1970-1975
Land Rover 1948-1973
Lotus Elan 1962-1973
Lotus Elan Collection No. 1
Lotus Europa 1966-1975
Lotus Seven 1958-1980
Maserati 1965-1970
Maserati 1970-1975
Mazda RX-7 Collection No. 1
Mercedes Benz Cars 1949-1954
Mercedes Benz Cars 1954-1957
Mercedes Benz Cars 1957-1961
Mercedes Benz Competition Cars 1950-1957
MG Cars in the 30's
MG Cars 1929-1934
MG Cars 1935-1940
MG Cars 1940-1947
MG Cars 1948-1951
MG Cars 1952-1954
MG Cars 1955-1957
MG Cars 1957-1959
MG Cars 1959-1962
MG Midget 1961-1979
MG MGA 1955-1962
MG MGB 1962-1970
MG MGB 1970-1980
MG MGB GT 1965-1980
Mini-Cooper 1961-1971
Morgan 3-Wheeler 1930-1952
Morgan Cars 1936-1960
Morgan Cars 1960-1970
Morgan Cars 1969-1979
Morris Minor 1949-1970
Nash Metropolitan 1954-1961
Packard Cars 1920-1942
Pantera 1970-1973
Pantera & Mangusta 1969-1974
Pontiac GTO 1964-1970
Pontiac Firebird 1967-1973
Porsche Cars 1952-1956
Porsche Cars 1957-1960
Porsche Cars 1960-1964
Porsche Cars 1964-1968
Porsche Cars 1968-1972
Porsche Cars 1972-1975
Porsche Cars in the 60's
Porsche 914 1969-1975
Porsche 911 Collection No. 1
Porsche 928 Collection No. 1
Porsche Turbo Collection No. 1
Riley Cars 1932-1935
Riley Cars 1936-1939
Riley Cars 1940-1945
Riley Cars 1945-1950
Riley Cars 1950-1955
Rolls Royce Cars 1930-1935
Rolls Royce Cars 1935-1940
Rolls Royce Cars 1940-1950
Rover P4 1949-1959
Rover P4 1955-1964
Singer Sports Cars 1933-1954
Studebaker Cars 1923-1939
Sunbeam Alpine & Tiger 1959-1967
Triumph Spitfire 1962-1980
Triumph Stag 1970-1980
Triumph TR2 & TR3 1952-1960
Triumph TR4 & TR5 1961-1969
Triumph GT6 1966-1974
TVR 1960-1980
Volkswagen Cars 1935-1956
VW Beetle 1956-1977
Volvo 1800 1960-1973
Volvo 120 Series 1956-1970

CONTENTS

ACKNOWLEDGEMENTS

A casual glance at our current list of titles on page two will reveal that we have published three previous books on the XKE (known as the E-Type in Europe) which might seem adequate coverage for a vehicle that was built in modest numbers over fourteen years.

Brooklands Books prime objective however is to try and make available to today's owners of interesting cars all the important articles that were published during their production life, hence this fourth book.

The E-Type Jaguar is an excellent example of an interesting car, it is one that must be preserved at all cost as fast powerful open sports cars are all too rapidly disappearing from our roads. When compiling the previous books we were forced reluctantly to omit many excellent XKE articles due to lack of space, happily with the support of Jaguar owners we can now return to the subject and offer this supplement to those three earlier titles.

These road tests, reports and driving impressions are of course copyright. The original publishers generously allow their reproduction in small numbers for the benefit of owners, historians, collectors and enthusiasts and I am sure that Jaguar devotees will wish to join with me in thanking the management of Autocar, Autosport, Car, Car & Driver, Cars and Car Conversions (previously Cars Illustrated), Modern Motor, Motor, Motor Sport, Road Test, Sporting Motorist and Sports Car World for their kindness and understanding. We are indebted to Paul Skilleter for supplying the attractive cover photograph.

R.M. Clarke

March 15 1961

Announcing

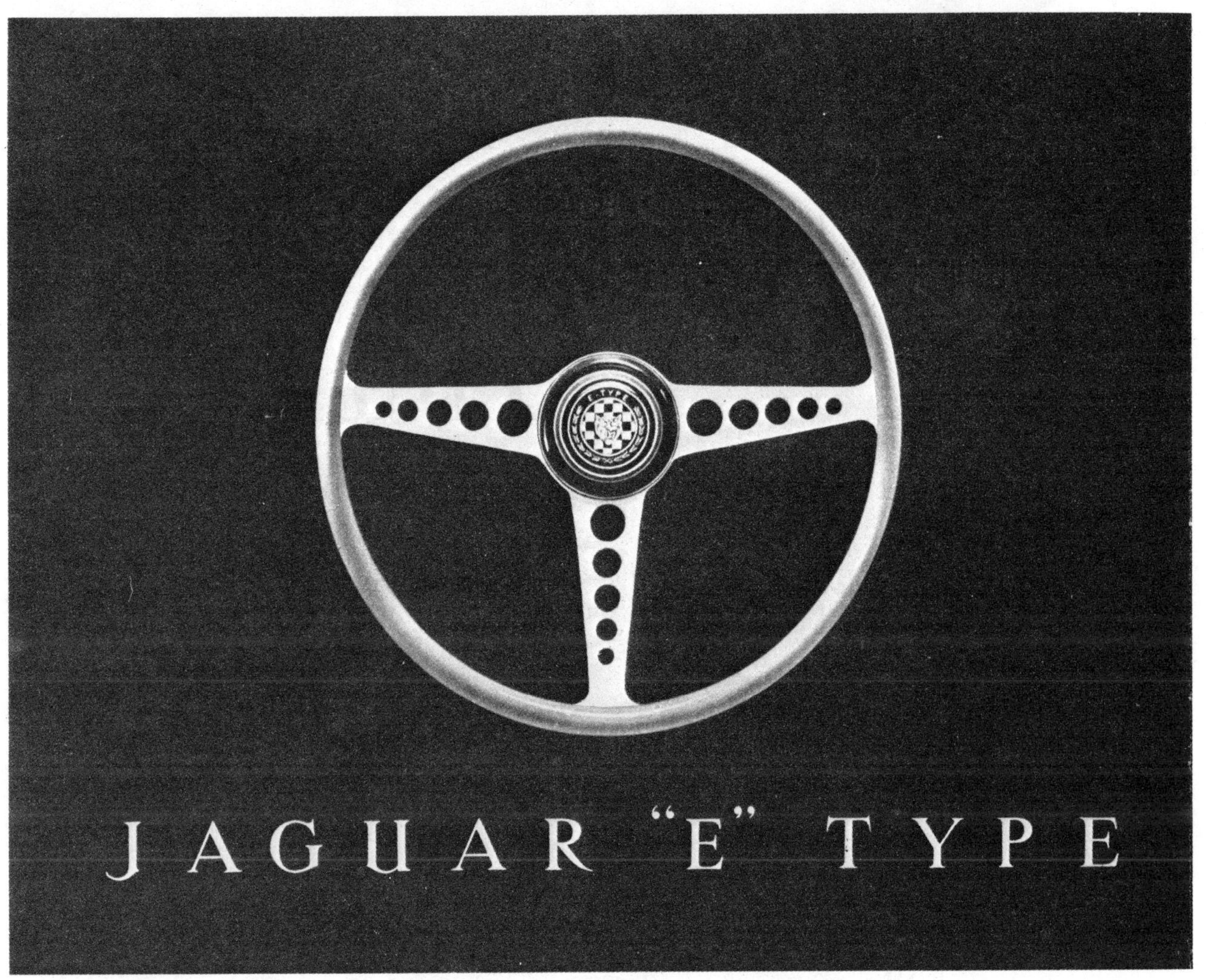

the most advanced
sports car
in the world

1961 CARS

The New 150 m.p.h. JAGUAR

FIRST FULL DESCRIPTION OF THE E-TYPE GRAND TOURING MODELS

THE PRICES

	Basic	*Total with P.T.*
Open two-seater	£1,480	£2,097 15s. 10d.
Detachable hardtop	£54	£76 10s. 0d.
Fixed-head coupé	£1,550	£2,196 19s. 2d.

FULL details can now be made public of the new E-type Grand Touring Jaguar after months of rumours here and abroad that the Coventry company had such a car in active development. With a maximum speed of approximately 150 m.p.h. in standard trim, the new Jaguar marks a big step forward in performance. Nevertheless, it should be stressed that the E-type is not intended as a sports-racing car (although some owners will doubtless use their cars in that way), but as a practical means of high-speed everyday transport suited to the needs of both sports enthusiasts and business or professional motorists who require to be as nearly in two places at once as modern engineering can devise.

The main features of the E-type are the well-tried XK engine in 3.8-litre, 265 b.h.p. "S" form, conventional synchromesh transmission, all-independent suspension, disc brakes and a combination of stressed-shell body construction allied to a tubular space-frame type of front end carrying the engine, front suspension and forward-hinged nose. With a dry weight of only 22 cwt. for the two-seater, unusually good aerodynamic shape and the power quoted above, the exceptional performance is readily understood. Detail points of unusual interest include a thermostatically controlled, electrically driven cooling fan and a new type of Lucas fuel pump submerged in the petrol tank.

The E-type is offered both as an open two-seater (for which a detachable hardtop is available) and as a two-seater fixed-head coupé. These models are introduced as additions to the current Jaguar range and do not supersede the existing XK150 models.

* * *

To begin with the basic structure, this is entirely new, although bearing obvious evidence of previous experience with the D-type. The main portion takes the form of a welded, stressed shell built up almost entirely of 20-gauge steel sheet.

The method of construction is shown in an accompanying drawing from which it will be seen that its strength comes largely from the mating series of large box sections. At the front, a horse-shoe-shaped box surrounds the scuttle, its ends joined to deep hollow sills which, in turn, link with a substantial hollow member passing across the car just forward of the rear suspension. At floor level, the deep propeller-shaft tunnel (the rear portion of which is fully enclosed) and a square-section transverse member form a linking cross with the scuttle, the sills and the rear box member, the latter in turn mated with longitudinal, inverted-top-hat sections which are welded to the boot floor and provide a mounting for the rear suspension/final-drive unit. Further longitudinal top-hat sections are welded to the underside of the cockpit floor.

In addition to the strength provided by these box sections, the panels contribute still further to the rigidity of the whole as almost without exception they are of curved formation.

At the front, a part-welded, part-bolted structure of Reynolds 541 square-section steel tubing forms a sub-frame which carries the engine, front suspension and forward-hinged nose. This sub-frame is in three sections—two side assemblies and a front transverse assembly—each of welded construction, but bolted together to form a whole which, in turn, is bolted to the main

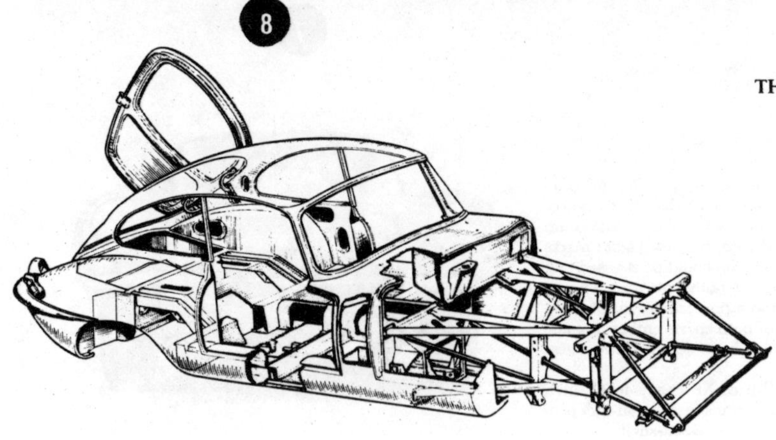

BASIC STRUCTURE of the new E-type. The stressed-shell main portion obtains its strength largely from the deep box sections of the body sills, propeller-shaft tunnel and cross members (including the horse-shoe-shaped scuttle), but additional rigidity is given by inverted top-hat sections welded to the floor and by the curvature of the panels. The front tubular structure, which carries the engine, suspension and front-hinged nose, is detachable. The open model is similar apart from the head and opening rear panel.

shell. Thus major overhauls or accident repair are facilitated; also, the whole front-hinged nose piece consists of three panels—two sides and the centre piece—which are bolted together with the joint concealed by a chromium-plated moulding.

The front suspension—by means of torsion bars and wishbones of unequal length—follows D-type practice rather than XK150 design in that the torsion bars are mounted in inner extensions of the lower wishbones instead of in the wishbone pivots. This arrangement, which results in the torsion bars bending slightly as well as twisting, enables them to be removed without disturbing the remainder of the suspension. As at the rear, an anti-roll bar is provided.

The principal advantages of independent rear suspension are well known, namely improved wheel adhesion owing to the absence of weight transference effects under driving torque, reduction of unsprung weight (with further adhesion and road-holding advantages in both driving and braking conditions, as well as increased comfort) and (dependent on the geometry adopted) increased cornering power. It is of interest that E-type independent rear suspension was fitted to a Mark 2 Jaguar for development work and showed a reduction of no less than 190 lb. (more than 50%) in unsprung weight compared with the standard solid axle.

Although the E-type layout differs in a number of important respects from that of the special experimental car entered at Le Mans last year by Briggs Cunningham, an examination of the design shows that much of the development work on that car has borne fruit on the E-type. On the new car, however, the final drive unit, the inboard disc brakes and the half-shafts and hub carriers are all assembled, together with the suspension elements, to form a virtually self-contained unit carried by a massive bridge-piece fabricated from steel pressings.

This bridge-piece is attached to the underside of the body structure via a pair of V-disposed rubber mountings on each side, and as both the anti-roll bar and the longitudinal radius arms are also attached by rubber mounting points to the body structure, the result is to eliminate all metal-to-metal contact between the final-drive/suspension unit and the body, thus isolating the latter completely from high-frequency transmission and road vibrations.

Equally important is the fact that the V-disposition of the rubber mounting points above the axle, coupled with the special rubber mountings at the forward ends of the radius arms (which permit a slight expansion and contraction of their effective length) are designed to allow a controlled degree of rotational movement of the axle casing—actually a maximum of 5 degrees under driving torque and 3 degrees under braking. The result (which corresponds roughly to the movement permitted to a solid axle mounted on semi-elliptic springs) is to provide a cushion effect and cut out transmission judder.

The Final Drive

A Salisbury 4HU hypoid-bevel final drive unit incorporating a Powr-Lok differential is used, its casing rigidly mounted at top and sides in the bridge member, and a pair of universally jointed tubular half-shafts convey the drive to the hubs. Needle-roller universal joints which require no lubrication are used and, because the half-shafts also serve as the upper suspension links, no sliding joints are employed and the half-shafts are of large diameter. To cater for transverse loads, taper-roller bearings are used at both ends of the half-shafts and the hubs themselves are housed in light-alloy castings which are extended downwards to provide pivot points for the lower links which are below, and parallel with, the half-shafts.

The lower links take the form of single tubular members of 2½ in. outside diameter with fork-shaped forged ends providing widely spaced bearings. At the inner ends, the bearings are of the double needle-roller type spaced approximately 11 in. apart, whilst approximately 5 in. separates the taper-roller bearings used at the outer ends. Connecting the axle ends of the radius arms (and also rubber mounted) is an anti-roll bar.

As will be seen from the drawings, the coil springs (which embrace Girling hydraulic dampers) are duplicated on each side, the idea, of course, being to economize space, as the two springs can be accommodated one on each side of the half-shaft. They are mounted on lugs on the tubular lower links, with upper

(*Continued on page 247*)

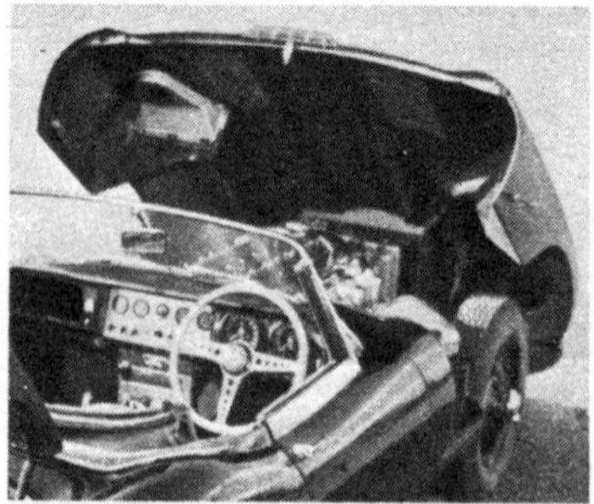

IMPRESSIVELY LONG, the bonnet (made in three pieces), is hinged near the front for access to the engine.

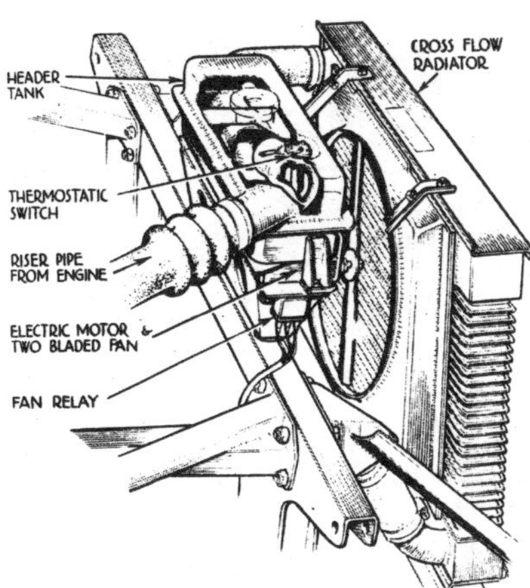

COOLING INNOVATIONS on the E-type include an electrically-driven fan which operates only when required and is brought into action by a thermostatic switch located in the water flow from the cylinder head. The flow is ducted through the header tank which serves merely to provide for expansion and contraction.

FRONT END details of the E-type shown in this sketch of a left-hand drive model include the arrangement of the torsion i.f.s., the rack-and-pinion steering, the disc brakes and the reservoirs for the hydraulic clutch operation and for the twin brake master cylinders. Connections for the warning lights for the brake reservoirs can be seen and also the top of the Dunlop mechanical booster. The engine is the 3.8-litre "S" type.

The New 150 m.p.h. JAGUAR

and noise. On the E-type, a Lucas 3 GM motor is used and is controlled by a thermostatic switch in the header tank which (with a tolerance of plus or minus 2 degrees F.) is designed to switch on the motor when the temperature of the water from the head reaches 80 degrees F. and to switch it off when the temperature falls to 73 degrees F. The motor, which drives a slender two-bladed fan located in a cowl, runs at approximately 2,300 r.p.m. and consumes 6-7 amp.

Further points of interest in the cooling system are the way in which the hot water from the head is directed within the header tank to the outlet, only a small gap between the internal ducts allowing for contraction and expansion. The radiator is of the cross-flow type and air to it is ducted direct from the nose of the car, other ducts providing cool air for the carburetters and fresh air for the body heating and ventilation system.

Completing the mechanical features of the E-type are a normal Borg and Beck single-dry-plate clutch and the remote-control Jaguar gearbox which has been used for many years past.

To turn now to the coachwork, both bodies are pure two-seaters, with no attempt at occasional seating. There is a useful space behind the separately adjustable seats for small parcels and this is partitioned off in the case of the open model, which has a separate boot with a normal front-hinged lid. The depth of the luggage space is naturally somewhat restricted by the low build of the car and the presence of the tank and spare wheel beneath the near-flat floor.

In the fixed-head coupé, considerably greater luggage space is available owing to the sweep of the roof, and a hinged luggage retainer at the front of the boot can be swung down to increase the floor area if required. The rear of the body is reached through a large side-hinged panel which contains the sharply sloping rear window.

Seating dimensions are the same in both cases, key dimensions being a shoulder width between doors of 49 in., a fore-and-aft cushion measurement of 20 in., and headroom of 35 in. The front-hinged doors extend below the deep, sharply raked windscreen, which has a very pronounced wrap-round and is provided with a new two-speed Lucas screenwiper with three blades. Thanks to thin pillars, vision is excellent and the winding windows (of both the open model and the coupé) disappear completely into the doors. The rear quarter lights of the coupé are hinged for ventilation.

The hood of the open car is designed for single-handed erection. Special attention has been paid to obtaining a good seal at the screen in the interests of both weather protection and high-speed security, and the forward portion of the mohair covering is reinforced by a metal plate; when furled, the hood is concealed by a detachable cover. A detachable glass-fibre hardtop is available, and, a good point this, the folded hood can be left in place when it is fitted.

As one expects from Jaguar, fittings and furnishings are comprehensive and of high quality. A three-panel facia board is used, with a large clear-faced 160 m.p.h. speedometer and matching rev. counter immediately in front of the driver, and the smaller dials (oil pressure, water temperature, fuel gauge and ammeter), together with labelled tumbler switches for the ancillary equipment, occupy the centre panel; the latter is hinged to give access to the wiring when required. On the passenger's side are an open glove locker and a grab handle. Other features in the very extensive range of equipment include a light-alloy steering wheel with wood rim, a fresh-air heating and demisting system, and provision for radio. In short, the term Grand Touring has a far wider meaning when applied to this new ultra-high-performance Jaguar than the somewhat narrow significance defined in the International Sporting Code.

ACCESS to luggage on the fixed-head model is provided from both within and without. Highlights on the body show the sweeping curves of the rear wing/rear quarter junction.

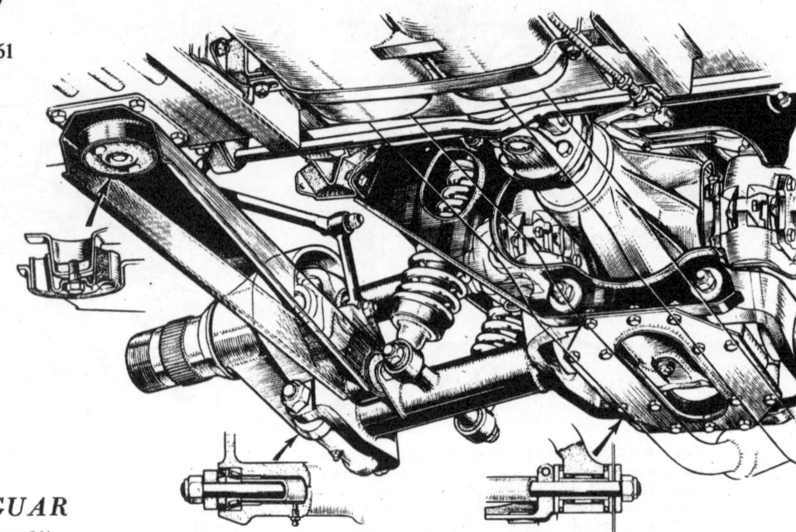

WORMS-EYE VIEW of the final drive and independent rear suspension. Points to note include the inboard Dunlop disc brakes, the twin coil springs on each side, and the way in which the half-shafts also serve as upper suspension links. Inset details show the special forward rubber mountings of the radius arms (see text), the taper roller bearings at the outer ends of the lower links and the double-needle-roller bearings used at the inner ends of these links.

The New 150 m.p.h. JAGUAR

(Continued from page 246)

abutments on the bridge member. Progressive rubber bump stops are used.

As the lower links are longer than the parallel half-shafts which form the upper links, the arrangement offers a compromise in which variations in camber and track are both restricted to a reasonable minimum. In the static condition, the roll centre is 5 $\frac{3}{16}$ in. above ground level and the camber angle $\frac{1}{2}$ to 1 degree negative. The geometry is such that variations in track have been virtually eliminated if one wheel hits a bump on roll, whilst the effect of roll on camber angle of the outer wheel is extremely small; as a result, the disturbing effects of road irregularities on corners are minimized and the cornering power of the tyre is not appreciably affected by adverse wheel camber.

Dunlop disc brakes are used all round and, as mentioned earlier, the rear discs are located inboard, with provision for cooling via a large aperture in the suspension bridge member. The callipers are forward mounted with the usual quick-change pads, and the separate hand-brake callipers are situated above, with an adjuster accessible from under the car.

Twin master cylinders with a compensating link of limited travel are used so that failure of the front brakes leaves the rear still in action and vice versa. Each master cylinder has its own reservoir and each is fitted with a low-level warning device, coupled to a single warning light on the facia panel. Servo assistance is given by the latest Dunlop bellows-type mechanical booster which was fully described in *The Motor* of December 28, 1960, and which has the advantage that no fluid seals are involved and that it is not necessary to bleed the hydraulic system if service to the booster is necessary.

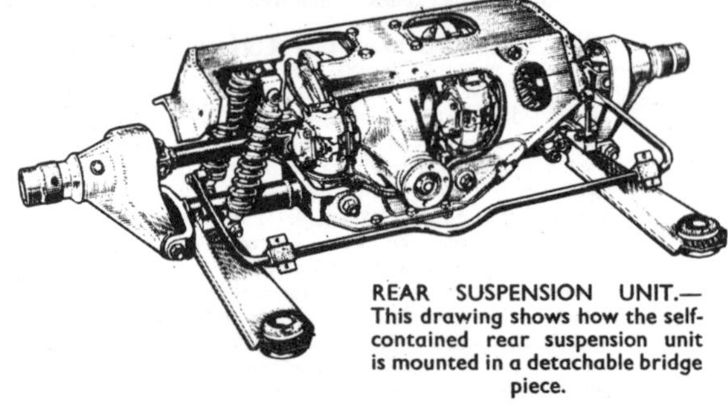

REAR SUSPENSION UNIT.—This drawing shows how the self-contained rear suspension unit is mounted in a detachable bridge piece.

So far little has been said about the engine because this is already well known, being the XK unit in its largest and most powerful form with "S" type head and twin exhausts, each with two silencers. A point of interest is that the three carburetters are fed from a horizontal rear tank beneath the boot floor by a new Lucas electric pump which is unusual in working completely immersed in the fuel. *This is fully described elsewhere in this issue (see P. 228).*

Another innovation on the E-type is the use of an electrically-driven cooling fan, also of new Lucas design. This has been fitted partly because it is easy to install, but also because a conventional engine-driven fan is a source of both power loss

JAGUAR E-TYPE SPECIFICATION

ENGINE	
Cylinders	6 in line with 7-bearing crankshaft.
Bore and stroke ...	87 mm. × 106 mm. (3.425 in. × 4.173 in.).
Cubic capacity ...	3,781 c.c. (230.64 cu. in.).
Piston area ...	55.28 sq. in.
Compression ratio	9/1 (8/1 optional).
Valvegear	Inclined o.h.v. operated by twin chain-driven overhead camshafts and located at included angle of 70 degrees in hemispherical combustion chambers in "straight port" aluminium-alloy cylinder head.
Carburation ...	Three type HD8, S.U. carburetters, fed by Lucas Model SFP pump located within 14-gallon tank.
Ignition	Lucas 12-volt coil, centrifugal and vacuum timing control, 14 mm. Champion N5 sparking plugs.
Lubrication ...	Tecalemit full-flow filter; sump capacity 11 pints (plus 2 for filter).
Cooling	Pressurized water cooling with pump, thermostat and electrically driven fan; 11-pint water capacity (incl. heater).
Electrical system ...	12-volt, 57 amp. hr. battery charged by 360-watt generator.
Maximum power ...	265 b.h.p. (gross) at 5,500 r.p.m., equivalent to 165 lb./sq. in. b.m.e.p. at 3,825 ft./min. piston speed and 4.8 b.h.p. per sq. in. of piston area.
Maximum torque ...	260 lb. ft. at 4,000 r.p.m., equivalent to 170 lb./sq. in. b.m.e.p. at 2,780 ft./min. piston speed.
TRANSMISSION	
Clutch	Borg and Beck 10-in. s.d.p., hydraulically operated.
Gearbox	Four-speed; with direct-drive top and synchromesh on 2nd, 3rd and top gears.
Overall ratios ...	3.31, 4.246, 6.156 and 11.177 (reverse 11.177). Alternative final-drive ratios: 2.93, 3.07 and 3.54.
Propeller shaft ...	Hardy Spicer open.
Final Drive... ...	Salisbury hypoid bevel with Powr-Lok limited-slip differential; casing attached to bridge member rubber mounted on body structure.
CHASSIS	
Brakes	Dunlop discs all round, inboard mounted at rear. Hydraulic operation by twin master cylinders. Dunlop bellows-type vacuum servo.
Brake dimensions	Fronts discs 11 in. dia.; rear, 10 in. dia.
Brake areas ...	31.8 sq. in. pad area working on 451 sq. in. rubbed area of discs. Front/rear braking ratio, 60/40.
Front suspension ...	Independent by torsion bars and unequal length ball-jointed wishbones; Girling telescopic dampers; anti-roll bar.
Rear suspension ...	Independent by twin coil springs each side incorporating Girling telescopic dampers; wheel location by parallel transverse links of unequal length (half-shafts acting as upper links) and longitudinal radius arms; anti-roll bar.
Wheels and tyres ...	Centre-lock wire wheels and 6.40-15 Dunlop RS5 tyres and tubes. Dunlop R5 racing tyres (6.00-15 front and 6.50-15 rear) available as optional extra on special wheels.
Steering	Rack and pinion, with adjustment for height and reach.
DIMENSIONS	
Length	Overall 14 ft. 7 $\frac{5}{16}$ in.; wheelbase 8 ft. 0 in.
Width	Overall 5 ft. 5 $\frac{1}{4}$ in.; track 4 ft. 2 in.
Height	Coupé, 4 ft. 0 $\frac{1}{8}$ in.; 2-str. and hard top, 3 ft. 10 $\frac{1}{2}$ in. Ground clearance 5 $\frac{1}{2}$ in.
Turning circle ...	37 ft.
Kerb weight ...	Coupé, 22 $\frac{1}{2}$ cwt.; 2-str. 22 cwt. (without fuel but with oil, water, tools, spare wheel, etc.). Front/rear weight distribution, driver only, 50/50; fully laden, 46/54.
EFFECTIVE GEARING*	
Top gear ratio ...	22.8 m.p.h. at 1,000 r.p.m. and 32.8 m.p.h. at 1,000 ft. min. piston speed.
Maximum torque ...	4,000 r.p.m. corresponds to approx. 91-92 m.p.h. in top gear.
Maximum power	5,500 r.p.m. corresponds to approx. 126 m.p.h. in top gear.
Probable top gear pulling power ...	500 lb./ton approx. (Computed by *The Motor* from manufacturers' figures for torque, gear ratio and kerb weight, with allowances for 3 $\frac{1}{2}$ cwt., load, 10% losses and 60 lb./ton drag.)

**Note.*—These calculations apply to the coupé model fitted with the Dunlop RS5 tyres supplied as standard and the normal 3.31/1 axle ratio; they have been worked out on the rolling radius at 30 m.p.h., tyre growth at high speeds having been ignored for this purpose.

Continued from page 66

Bumps don't affect it but strong side winds make the long nose dither a bit at times, an effect probably emphasised visually because it is so long, and hardly noticed through the steering.

High speed bumps are taken with ease but there is some bumping about on the low-speed, short-pitched ripple type of going. Cornering roll is low but handling a trifle long in the tooth.

Because of the fat tyres, Jaguar has found it necessary to supply power steering as standard and although it does manage to be heavier than that of the XJ6 it is still frighteningly light for such a handleable, fast car. Putting at least some feel in the steering would also make slide correction more a matter of seat-of-pants driving than simply applying what you think are the correct settings, as it is now. There must be a fortune awaiting the designer who can produce power steering with a rate-of-assistance control on the dashboard so that individual drivers can select what they want. Obviously, many (including the Jaguar designers) are happy with so much lightness. But have the factory people become too used to driving XJ6s? An enthusiast who drove the E would immediately say yes.

From the steering point of view, the E-type is no longer a sports car, but a long-range fast cruiser in the original meaning of GT.

And if we accept this, then the interior fittings must cop a host of criticism.

For example, though there are flow-through outlets in the hardtop, there is still no face-level ventilation, yet this *is* 1972. And it is high time that Jaguar listened to its critics and sorted out the switchery. What may be easily understood by a telephone switchboard operator or a driver used to the car isn't good enough when you have 150 mph performance. You shouldn't have switches that have to be read before you are sure you're operating the correct one.

As for the dipswitch protruding from the fascia like an afterthought and separate wiper and washer switches on the left instead of being on the column for instant use at speed . . . anyone who has hit an unexpected thundershower at speed will realise the need for fingertip control of the wipers.

There is now plenty of seat adjustment and the front seats are comfortable, if not over-generous in sideways location. But there is still need of somewhere to rest the left foot.

You can throw a lot of junk on the space behind the seats but the boot of the roadster is small, with little over four cubic ft of usable space. All-round vision is surprisingly good.

At 15 miles to the gallon, the 18-gal tank is just about big enough.

The fact of the matter is that the E-type, one of the classic cars of all time, has now got down right elderly and while the new engine has given it a shot in the arm, the next step must surely be a new body (and the word is that that's the case) to take full advantage of the mechanical parts.

By today's standards, far too much width is wasted in tumble-home side panelling, and others have shown that it is possible to build a strong chassis without sidewalls to climb over.

The life span of a good car design is much the same as that of a cat, and this particularly pussy is nearing the end.

It will catch a lot of mice yet, that's for sure, and it purrs more sweetly than ever before — but somewhere on a drawing board there must be a kitten near weaning, ready to take over the queen's crown.

*

E-TYPE IS HERE!

(Continued from page 14)

from inside, is shallow, but will accommodate a quantity of soft luggage. The coupe version, of course, offers far more luggage space, in the manner of DB 2/4 Astons.

On the Road

Driving the "E"-type is a joy which all Jaguar fans should be allowed. It's so unlike any other Jaguar—except perhaps the "D"—in handling, steering and ride comfort.

Yet, if you were blindfolded, the car's docile smoothness could be mistaken for that of a 3.8 saloon or Mark IX. It is entirely tractable, pottering along in top as low as 10 m.p.h., and surging forward at the smallest increase in throttle opening.

As the "E" had just come off the ship and had only 19 miles up, I kept under 3000 r.p.m.—but this was enough to bring 75 up on the speedo with the 3.3 to 1 final gearing. At that speed there was very little noise either from engine or exhausts, and wind or road sounds were almost nil.

The "E" makes all other sports or semi-sports cars seem noisy, uncomfortable, and, I suppose, slow. It felt as though glued to the road, and the ride was wonderfully smooth, without any trace of shudder or bounce, even on ripply bitumen.

Although tyre pressures were too low for a fair test, I failed to induce any breakaway when forcing the "E" into a downhill sweeping corner. The steering, with 2½ light turns from lock to lock, was delightful; it has obviously received special attention from Jaguar engineers, for high-speed accuracy, though essential, is by no means found on all fast cars.

Brakes, of course, are superb—for with its low-drag body and high speed, the "E" simply must have the best. Dunlop discs are mounted all round, with quick-change pads.

Separate hydraulic systems front and rear are an added safety factor, and each master-cylinder has its own reservoir, plus a low-level warning system which operates a red light on the dash.

Servo-assistance is very effective, calling for only light pedal pressures, even for maximum braking.

Apart from my dislike of the gearbox—and perhaps those tizzy bits of green plastic covering the trafficator warning lights on the dash—the E-type left me full of enthusiasm.

It is probably the best example of what we have all longed for: a true dual-purpose car, suitable for town and country, and a formidable opponent to face at any race meeting.

And all this will be available for much less than you'd have to pay for any other thoroughbred G.T. car.

Most speculations concerning the E-type's Australian price plumped for £4000 including tax — but **Modern Motor** hit the nail on the head by predicting, last May, that the open car would cost £3500 and the coupe £3700.

The £3500 prediction was right on the mark; the coupe's price is still to be finalised, but Brysons say it will cost "up to £250" more.

I can't think of any other car that offers better value for money.

E-TYPE IS HERE!

Fabulous new Jaguar has reached Australia sooner than expected. It does 150 m.p.h., handles magnificently —yet costs less than a Mk. 9 saloon, reports David McKay

AUSTRALIA has received its first two E-type Jaguars — a white open two-seater which I have just driven in Sydney, and a sister-car for Melbourne.

Neither has a definite owner as yet: they have been imported primarily for show purposes by the Jaguar agents, Bryson Industries.

The Sydney car was originally intended for me, but the factory graciously offered to prepare a coupe for competition work which, I hope, won't be too long coming.

My first impression of the open "E" was decidedly mixed. It is a glorious car, lovely from any angle and looking even better than its pictures.

But while admiring it, I couldn't help thinking what a lethal weapon it could be in irresponsible hands.

As it stood before me, it was capable of 150 m.p.h. and could turn up "the ton" in 16 seconds. Not that

BEAUTY and efficiency blend in the E-type's wind-tunnel-designed shape. From low-entry nose to kicked-up tail, everything is calculated to cut drag.

the "E" is difficult to drive—it's easier and safer than any other Jaguar, and a sensible even if inexperienced driver would be no more of a road hazard in it than a careful "Auntie" in her Morris Minor.

But irresponsibility mixed with the "E" even in small doses would produce a deadly combination.

The Jaguar Car Company claims its E-type Grand Touring models are the most advanced cars in the world. If they added the word "production," it would be impossible to argue against this claim.

Their literature reads: "No more famous background can be found"—"fast, elegant and luxuriously appointed road vehicles" — "offers a performance in which ultra-rapid acceleration and high maximum speeds are matched by superlative braking power and the highest degree of controllability" — "extraordinarily high safety factor . . ."

Many car manufacturers have made extravagant claims for their products over the years, but these statements by Jaguar are mere fact.

Body and "Works"

Let's look at the "E." It comes in two models — the fixed-head coupe and the open car, which can be fitted with an optional fibreglass hardtop without removing the folded soft hood.

The whole design follows the D-type competition car as closely as possible, particularly with regard to the stressed-skin body shell and the tubular-steel subframes carrying the engine and front end, also the rear suspension and final drive unit.

All body panels are load-carrying in this design, which gives maximum stiffness in relation to lightness. The front subframe, of square-section tube, is bolted to the main body; its components, too, are bolted together, so that a damaged member can be replaced without welding.

You get first-class engine accessibility (never before a strong point with Jaguars), thanks to the forward-hinged, one-piece bonnet-and-wings assembly.

This reveals the renowned six-cylinder XK double-overhead-camshaft engine, which in its latest "S" form delivers 265 b.h.p. at 5500 r.p.m., and 260 lb./ft. torque at 4000.

Compression is 9 to 1, and 100-octane petrol MUST be used. I understand an aluminium block is in the offing, to help offset the weight problem Jaguar must overcome before tackling the very special Ferrari Berlinettas at Le Mans.

The new cooling system will interest those Jaguar owners who have

XK "S"-type engine with three carbs delivers 265 b.h.p. in standard form. One-piece bonnet-and-wings assembly allows easy access.

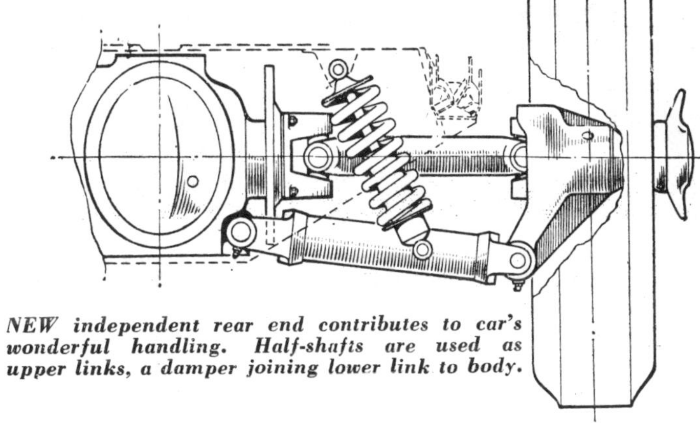

NEW independent rear end contributes to car's wonderful handling. Half-shafts are used as upper links, a damper joining lower link to body.

MAIN SPECIFICATIONS

ENGINE: 6-cylinder, d.o.h.c.; bore 87mm., stroke 106mm., capacity 3781c.c.; compression ratio 9 to 1; maximum b.h.p. 265 at 5500 r.p.m.; maximum torque 260ft./lb. at 4000 r.p.m.; 3 SU carburettors, electrical fuel pump; 12v. ignition.

TRANSMISSION: Single dry-plate hydraulic clutch; 4-speed gearbox synchromeshed on top three; ratios—1st and reverse 3.777; 2nd 1.86; 3rd 1.283; top 1 to 1; limited slip differential.

SUSPENSION: Independent all round; front by wishbones and torsion bars; twin coil springs at rear; telescopic hydraulic shock-absorbers all round.

STEERING: Rack-and-pinion; 2½ turns lock-to-lock; 37ft. turning circle.

BRAKES: Servo-assisted Dunlop discs.

WHEELS: 72-spoke wire with knock-off hubs and Dunlop RS5 6.40 by 15in. tyres.

CONSTRUCTION: Unitary.

DIMENSIONS: Wheelbase 8ft. 0in.; track (front and rear) 4ft. 2in.; length 14ft. 7¼in., width 5ft. 5in., height 4ft. 0in.; ground clearance 5in.

KERB WEIGHT: 21cwt.

FUEL TANK: 14 gallons.

CLAIMED PERFORMANCE

STANDING quarter-mile: 14.8s.

ACCELERATION from rest through gears: 0-60, 7.0s.; 0-100, 16.0s.

ACCELERATION in top: 10-30, 5.7s.; 20-40, 5.2s.; 30-50, 5.3s.; 40-60, 5.0s.; 50-70, 5.4s.; 60-80, 5.3s.; 70-90, 5.5s.; 80-100, 5.7s.; 90-100, 6.3s.; 100-120, 8.2s.

NOTE: Factory figures taken at England's M.I.R.A. testing ground in wet conditions.

(These performance figures are for the open model—but as the coupe weighs only 56lb. more, its times should be very close.)

PRICE: £3500 including tax

BUCKET seats hold you steady on corners, all controls and instruments are ideally placed. But it's time Jaguar built a new gearbox, says McKay.

sat unhappily in summer traffic jams while their beloved engines boiled.

The "E" uses an electric fan to ensure a high rate of airflow at low speeds; this is switched on thermostatically at 80deg. centigrade and cuts out as temperature drops to 72deg., to avoid wasting power.

A high-efficiency cross-flow radiator is fitted to the subframe, and a separate header tank is mounted just forward of the engine.

Power is transmitted from the engine via a 10-inch single dry-plate, hydramatically-operated clutch to a four-speed gearbox.

It is here that the "E" disappoints, for the old box is just not good enough for such a car. It is robust, but lacks synchro on first and a quick, light movement.

A longer lever would help, but the only answer is an entirely new box, which Jaguar will doubtless produce later, probably saving a bit more weight at the same time.

A short tailshaft takes the drive to the hypoid differential, carried in a subframe, together with the rear suspension.

Interesting Rear End

While the front end follows the familiar D-type design of transverse wishbones and torsion bars, the rear suspension is entirely new.

To me this is the biggest feature of the new car—and the factory says it makes the car "a revelation to handle."

This suspension uses the half-shafts as upper links, while the lower links (also tubular) not only form the lower supports in the vertical plane but also protect the stub-carriers from torsional movement.

Fore-and-aft movement is controlled by radius arms which run forward from the outer ends of the lower links to the rear box-section cross-member at the back of the body.

The whole assembly—suspension, differential casing, inboard disc brakes and mountings for the lower wishbones —is carried in a single fabricated subframe, supported at its outer ends on "V" rubber mountings located in the body frame, directly over the rear axle.

The idea of this flexibly mounted rear-axle unit is to eliminate all harshness of drive, as well as the road and transmission vibrations and noises which usually go hand-in-hand with independent rear suspension.

Cockpit, Equipment

Inside the "E," it is obvious that Jaguar have made use of all their experience in high-speed motoring. Thin pillars and wide wraparound screen give excellent vision over the bulging bonnet, and the bucket seats are placed high enough for the driver to feel in command.

The new wood-and-alloy racing wheel is adjustable for both height and reach, and I soon found the ideal driving position, with even a place for my clutch foot.

A full set of instruments keeps the driver informed; but although the speedo and tacho are well placed in front of the wheel, I still find them cluttered with figures and in need of redesigning.

Dash layout, apart from the absence of woodwork, is similar to the Mark II saloons. The headlights embody flash signals for overtaking, and the dipper switch is finger-operated.

Two-speed, triple-bladed wipers and electric screen-washers should cope with anything but utterly impossible weather conditions.

Although everything is functional, the usual Jaguar luxury is still there, with fine leather upholstery and pile carpets over thick underfelt. Individual fresh-air heating and demisting is also supplied.

Being of average height and build, I found the "E" had plenty of space—but very tall or very fat men may think it a tighter fit.

Luggage space is very fair for this type of car. The boot, opened

Continued on page 11

REAR view is lovely, too—and there's fair luggage space under that lid.

SPORTS CAR WORLD, October, 1963

CHRIS BECK DRIVES . . .

JAGUAR'S EXOTIC E

A full road test of the E-type Jaguar, a stimulating siren capable of 150 mph.

TO an Englishman nothing conjures up a picture of speed in the world of fast motoring more readily than the name Jaguar. During the last 10 years this famous firm, founded as the Swallow Sidecar Company in 1922 by Sir William Lyons, has become synonymous with high speed sedans and even faster sports cars. As value for performance they are almost unbeatable.

Jaguar first entered sports car racing in a big way in 1951 with a special competition model, designated the C-type, and proceeded to scoop the pool. That year they won the Le Mans Grand Prix d'Endurance, and the British Tourist Trophy, held on the open Dundrod circuit in Northern Ireland. Both times the distance and fastest lap records fell. In 1952 the cars retired from Le Mans with overheating problems because of a fault in the radiator design, but they won the arduous and gruelling Rheims Grand Prix at an average of 98 mph.

Again in 1953 Jaguars took first, second, fourth and ninth places at Le Mans, also raising the lap and distance records. This was the first race at the Sarthe circuit to be won at an average of over 100 mph. That year Jaguar reigned supreme in sports car racing, taking the Rheims GP, the

Using the world-famous XK twin overhead cams haft 265 bhp motor the car reached 146 mhp on test.

JAGUAR'S EXOTIC E . . . Continued

Hyeres 12 hours race and the Nurburgring 1000 kilometres.

Back in Coventry the Jaguar competition department was already that the C-type was fast becoming obsolete and early in 1954 the memorable and history-making D-type was unveiled. Although suspension, bodywork and chassis were vastly different the running gear in both models remained basically the same.

Power was provided by the stalwart twin overhead camshaft XK motor, developed from the motor used in the XK120 sports car put in production in 1947. At this stage it was producing more than 250 reliable bhp. The D-type used the same Moss gearbox as the C, but it was now fully synchronised. Bodywork was the result of intensive wind tunnel tests and as well as being highly efficient it had a masculine, eye-pleasing outline; it was probably the most appealing and handsome British sports car of its era.

That year Jaguar did not win the 24 heures du Mans, but finished a rewarding second. The Rheims GP was a Jaguar benefit, with team cars finishing first and second. In 1955 the team cars took out Le Mans, the British TT, the Sebring International and the Ulster Trophy Race, and each time lap or distance records fell.

Ecurie Ecosse took over the team cars when Jaguar withdrew from racing at the end of 1955. Under the guidance of David Murray, patron of the Ecurie, the now-ageing D-types romped home to win at Sarthe in 1956 and 1957.

From the stunningly successful D-type the XKSS was evolved as a road version. Only 300 were made before a disastrous fire swept through the body building section of the factory in 1957.

Production of the XKSS was stopped by the fire, but the company realised there was a market for a super-fast sports car and set to work on a car similar to the D-type, but including all the latest refinements.

In the spring of 1961 Jaguar announced the world's first genuine 150 mph quantity-production sports car — the E-type. It caused an immediate sensation.

In its attractive profile the E shows a wind-tunnel heritage. Windows must be kept up at speed.

A comprehensive array of instruments and well-labelled switches help tame this wild beast.

The E is what is known as Instant Success. It retained the best features of the D-type, but replaced the live rear axle with a fully independent system. Power was upped from 250 to 265 bhp by several minor modifications to the engine.

Recently SPORTS CAR WORLD was able to borrow one of these spectacular cars for a complete road test — the coupe of top nationwide TV and radio personality John Laws.

It is true that many people feel that the beautifully sculpted body, with its flowing aerodynamic lines, produces a reaction of sheer sensual joy. If it could be said a car has "sex appeal" then the E-type just reeks of it.

The coupe version, because of its better form, is slightly faster and looks far better than the roadster. Finished in a silver-grey, the test car looked fit to carry a Peruvian playboy, a Melburnian millionaire, a Sydney socialite, or what you will.

Obviously related to the D-type, the front section seems to have the same basic lines, although it looks slimmer; this could be an optical illusion. The bonnet is louvred either side of the hump provided for the cam boxes of the 3781 cc motor. Sloping slightly, the roof ends abruptly at the chopped off tail which imparts a distinct odour of the Kamm theory — popular, it seems, from Coventry to Maranello. At the front there is a large semi-wrap around windscreen and the door windows and rear window provide excellent all-round vision.

During the test, acceleration and speed runs the car was creditably quiet, although above 120 mph wind noise was audible and progressively worsened until the top speed was reached; but even at its maximum the car was highly liveable.

The 3.8 litre twin overhead camshaft engine has both inlet and exhaust valves at an angle of 45 degrees. Fed by three two inch SU carburettors it develops a highly respectable 265 bhp at 5500 rpm, while maximum torque of 260 ft/lb is reached at 4000 rpm.

The cylinder head is an aluminium alloy casting and the camshafts, of chilled cast iron (which is highly wear resistant) are operated by duplex chains. Seven main bearings allow the motor to run freely to 6500 rpm, but in the interests of safety a 6000 rpm limit should be maintained in normal day to day driving. It is an axazingly willing engine, and will potter along at 25 mph in top gear without any trouble. Touch the GO pedal and it responds with a ferocity akin to the animal from which it got its name.

On test a rev ceiling of 5750 rpm was observed as it was found to be futile to go any higher in the range. Torque was excellent above 2000 rpm; below this figure the motor was still extremely tractable, but pickup was definitely slower, one of the hints of its competition ancestry.

Jaguar's XK motors are well-known for their high piston feet/minute factor, but this does not seem to impair their reliability, and capacity to absorb hard work and brutal punishment.

Synchromesh, however, must be a dirty word at the Jaguar factory because the Moss gearbox, fitted to all manually controlled cars, virtually has none. This was one of the car's weakest points. During our first acceleration runs changes were made slowly and deliberately to avoid snicking or grating the gears. After finding we were not getting there as quick as we should, "crash" changes were reluctantly used to obtain the desired results. The close ratios were a joy to use; second particularly had a lot of poke—good for 90 mph—and double declutching quickened downshifts considerably, not an annoying procedure when coming into a sharp corner hurriedly as it was easy to imagine oneself going down through the box approaching the hairpin at the end of Mulsanne Straight at Sarthe.

Another noticeable fault was the clutch—a 10 in single dry plate Borg and Beck unit—which slipped badly under severe usage. After two or three acceleration runs a little clutch slip was detected and this gradually worsened until it was possible to slip it while cruising along in third and top gears. In a race version of the car the unit would be quite out of place and again it is hard to see why such a well-made vehicle does not have a heavier duty competition-type clutch. Nonetheless, it was extremely easy to use and only fairly light pedal pressures were needed.

Inside, the car is magnificently appointed, with an array of instruments that would do a light aircraft justice. Sitting immediately in front of

"Don't look at me like that." The E-type is the most sensual sports car ever built by Jaguar.

the driver there is a three spoked, alloy wood-rimmed steering wheel with a plastic Jaguar boss in the centre. It is fully adjustable and I found the straight arms position, with hands at ten to two, ideal. A large 160 mph speedometer and electric tachometer sits in a binnacle through which runs the steering column. In the centre of the facia is a pressed aluminium panel housing further ancillary gauges.

Below these dials there is a row of switches which control the parking, tail and headlights, windscreen wipers (of which there are three), washers and sundry other electrical subsidiaries. Underneath these in the test car, in the gearshift console, there was an awfully expensive Blaupunkt radio equipped with an automatic aerial and self seeking tuning — a lovely £200 worth which sets off the redlined interior admirably.

Red leather bucket seats adjustable for both height and length hold the occupants with the utmost comfort; even during the hardest cornering, when the Gs were high, there was adequate support for the thighs and hips. Behind the seats there is a large parcel shelf on which several suit cases can be carried. Access can be easily gained to this by turning around in the cockpit or opening the rear boot-hatch. Deep pile carpeting covers the floors and bulkheads throughout.

Returning to the outside we noticed that the car was shod with Pirelli Rolle tyres (costing more than £23 each) designed for sustained speeds up to 160 mph. Wheels are of the wire-spoke variety, triple-laced with knock-on hubs.

Suspension front and rear is fully independent and does a really marvellous job. At the front a wishbone-coil-telescopic damper system is used, while at rear is a swing axle set-up utilising transverse links, two coil springs and telescopic dampers per side.

The system does its job very well and at low speeds the ride was most un-sports car-like — very soft and sedate — but it got progressively harsher until at 130 mph it was quite stiff. It was

Triple-laced wire wheels offer an amount of resiliency and carry Pirelli Rolle running shoes.

PERFORMANCE

Top speed average	146 mph
Fastest run	146 mph
Maximum, first	43 mph
Maximum, second	90 mph
Maximum, third	115 mph
Maximum, fourth	NA
Standing quarter mile average	15.0 seconds
Fastest run	14.9 seconds
0 to 30 mph	3.2 seconds
0 to 40 mph	4.6 seconds
0 to 50 mph	5.5 seconds
0 to 60 mph	7.1 seconds
0 to 70 mph	9.9 seconds
0 to 80 mph	12.4 seconds
0 to 90 mph	14.0 seconds
0 to 100 mph	16.9 seconds
0 to 110 mph	21.4 seconds
0 to 120 mph	27.3 seconds
0 to 130 mph	31.7 seconds
0 to 140 mph	47.0 seconds
0 to 150 mph	NA

	Top	Third
40 to 60 mph	7.8 seconds	5.3 secs
50 to 70 mph	7.8 seconds	5.5 secs
60 to 80 mph	7.7 seconds	5.6 secs

not choppy, merely firm, and at no time at speed did one feel at all uncomfortable.

Thrown into corners at speed it initially understeers, a distinctive trait with most British cars, and then moves to final oversteer that is not excessive and extremely easy to handle. A quick flick of the steering wheel brings lightning-like response and then the car drifts in an oversteer attitude. In long fast, sweeping curves it would be better to have the car assume a slight drift angle in understeer than to have a series of oversteering corrections.

It is doubtful if the roadholding is as good as the rigid axle D, but with refinements to the system, as made to Bob Jane's racing coupe and several fuel injected models running successfully in sports car races in Britain and on the Continent, it would be a hard car to beat on a long fast circuit. On smaller tighter circuits where roadholding is the dominating factor, these big, relatively heavy cars need a lot of work on the part of the driver and even then good Lotus Super Sevens can usually worry them.

In the performance vein, acceleration was sense deadening; it topped the 100 mph mark in under 17 sec, which puts it in the light dragster class. We found it was best to let the clutch out about 3000 rpm, let the motor die a little and then apply full throttle, so that the full torque and power characteristics could be used. The limited slip differential restricted wheelspin and the tyres merely chirped on take-off. On a clear stretch of highway it took us just two miles to wind the car out to its maximum of 146 mph and this was on a dull, cloudy, humid day with a slight headwind. Under ideal conditions there should be no trouble in obtaining a genuine 155 mph. The test car was fitted with the standard 3.31 diff ratio but with the 2.93 ratio a top speed of 170 mph is available.

To cope with all this performance Dunlop disc

(Continued on page 57)

JAGUAR'S EXOTIC E . . . Continued

Luggage space is confined to the floor section in the tail. The rear window opens for baggage.

70 to 90 mph	8.1	5.7
80 to 100 mph	7.6	5.9
90 to 110 mph	7.8	7.1
100 to 120 mph	9.9	NA
110 to 130 mph	12.2	NA
Brake fade resistance on test hill		98 percent
Fuel consumption, overall		17 mpg
Fuel consumption, cruising		20 mpg

SPECIFICATIONS

CHASSIS AND BODY DIMENSIONS:

Wheelbase	8 ft 0 in
Track, front	4 ft 2 in
Track, rear	4 ft 2 in
Ground clearance	5½ in
Turning circle	37 ft
Turns, lock to lock	2.5
Overall length	14 ft 7 in
Overall width	5 ft 5 in
Overall Height	4 ft 0 in

CHASSIS:

Steering, type	rack and pinion
Brake, type	discs, all round
Swept area	461 sq in

Suspension, front:
independent, wishbones, coil springs.
Suspension, rear:
independent, transverse links, coil springs.

Shock absorbers	telescopic
Tyre size	6.40 by 15
Weight	26 cwt
Fuel tank capacity	14 gals
Approx. cruising range	300 miles

ENGINE:

Cylinders	six, in line
Bore and stroke	87 mm by 106 mm
Cubic capacity	3781 cc
Compression ratio	9 to 1
Fuel requirement	100 octane
Valves	twin overhead camshafts
Maximum power	265 bhp at 5500 rpm
Maximum torque	260 ft/lb at 5000 rpm

TRANSMISSION:

Overall ratios:

First	11.17
Second (synchro)	6.15
Third (synchro)	4.24
Fourth (synchro)	3.31
Final drive	1 to 1

JAGUAR XKE
Most Overrated?

CORVETTE STING RAY
Just a Plastic Chevy?

For many years Jaguar offered the most performance for the dollar of any sports car in the world. Its competition record kept fans loyal and sales up. Then, in the United States, the Corvette V8 emerged to challenge Jaguar both on the track and on the street as a prestige personal automobile. A radical design change in 1961 brought Jag back strong in the glamour group although it hasn't been able to score in competition. So also has the Corvette been eclipsed in that department in spite of a similar re-design in 1962.

☐ Now we have two fast, sporting *Gran Turismo* coupes of approximately the same character which, comparably equipped, are within the same price bracket. They represent attainable luxury concepts for many people.

☐ Which car, Jaguar XKE or Corvette Sting Ray, deserves the most consideration from the buyer who seeks this type of transportation?

JAGUAR PRICES

■ One big factor which can complicate a selection is the number of equipment choices which are part and parcel of the Corvette. In the true Detroit manner there are stated options as long as a laundry list for a family of eight. On the other hand a Jaguar is a Jaguar is a Jaguar in the essentials and about all the purchaser can whittle off the nominal $6,000 ticket is $175 for the chrome wire wheels, $50 for tinted glass, $50 for white sidewalls, and $15 for seat belts.

☐ Let's first consider what you get for the money.

☐ In the main – although $6,000 is a good piece of change to spend on impulse buying – most cars of this type are sold with the load, but a stripped XKE Coupe can be had for $5,685 P.O.E. West Coast. The roadster lists at $5,585. Prices would be $60 less if you could prevent the distributor from attaching the 'optional' bumper overriders, but these seem to be affixed at the dock and you may as well live with them. Included, for these figures, are such items as 265 bhp engine, four speed fully synchronized gearbox, limited slip differential, center lock wire spoke wheels (painted), four wheel power-assisted disc brakes, rack-and-pinion steering, adjustable steering wheel, windshield washers, 3-speed wipers, wood-rimmed steering wheel, leather bucket seats, full instrument panel, padded sun visors, heater, courtesy and map lights.

☐ Incidentally, painted wire wheels, although stock, are a special order. All XKEs coming to the States have the chromed type and probably 95% are sold so equipped.

CORVETTE OPTIONS

■ The Sting Ray Coupe has a basic list price of $4,321.

• Jaguar front suspension is by forged control arms and torsion bars. Corvette uses stampings, coil springs.

• Twin overhead cam Six has been Jaguar's power for over fifteen years. Alternator is new in 1965 models.

The roadster is $4,106. For this sum the purchaser gets a 250 bhp engine, 3 speed transmission, heater, vinyl bucket seats, adjustable steering wheel, 4 wheel disc brakes, seat belts and courtesy lamps. This would also be a 'special order.' ROAD TEST shoppers could not find a dealer in the Los Angeles metropolitan area (including Harry Mann, the world's largest Corvette dealer) who could remember delivering such a car. However, for the $1,300 price differential between this and the basic XKE, practically all of the assorted extras which are found on the majority of Corvettes can be applied. Without many of them, the Corvette is not competitive except in road holding and braking — leaving aesthetics entirely out of the discussion.

☐ The first step up the Corvette ladder is an alternate transmission. Chevy's 3-speed isn't the worst box in the world — in fact it compares rather favorably with the transmission just abandoned by Jaguar, being just about as noisy and having a non-synchro first gear — but the gap between first gear ratio (2.58) and second (1.48) is rather wide for sporty driving and the necessity for coming to a complete stop before engaging low gear is a nuisance in a non-economy car. The choice is between a Powerglide (at $199) or the all-synchro four speed with 2.56, 1.91, 1.48 and 1.00 ratios, (for $188). Another four speed with close ratios, (2.20, 1.64, 1.28, 1.00) is available only with 365 and 375 bhp engines. Powerglide can be had only with the 250 and 300 bhp engines.

☐ Engine choice is next. Chevy's 327 cubic inch V8 with 4.00 inch bore and 3.25 inch stroke is the sole offering but it comes in four stages of tune, as indicated on the accompanying chart. The significant increase of 50 bhp from the standard engine to L-75 is not easily accounted for. Cam timing is the same and the only difference is in carburetion. A Carter WCFB 4 barrel with 1.43 inch venturis used on the standard engine and an aluminum Carter AFB with 1.56 inch primary and 1.68 inch secondary venturis comes with L-75.

☐ The next option, L-76, has a number of changes: Cam, pistons, rings, bearings, valves, compression ratio, carburetion and exhaust system to justify its power increase. The L-84 gets it rating from the use of Rochester Fuel injection. Ten extra horsepower hardly seem to rate a $409 price differential, but if you intend to go into competition, the injected engine is mandatory because it is not affected by attitude whereas engines with this type of carburetor have a tendency to starve or flood (or both) under racing conditions.

☐ Although disc brakes are standard on all Corvettes, power is extra. This $43 item is not necessarily for little old ladies. Jag has servo-assist and the 'purists' approve it. Pedal pressure is high with disc brakes and, whether you are racing or touring, heavy application can be tiring.

CORVETTE ENGINE SPECIFICATIONS

Engine	Comp. Ratio	Carburetor	Torque	Horsepower
Standard	10.5 - 1	WCFB	350 @ 2,800	250 @ 4,400
RPO L 75	10.5 - 1	AFB	360 @ 3,200	300 @ 5,000
RPO L 76	11.0 - 1	Holley	350 @ 4,000	365 @ 6,200
RPO L 84	11.0 - 1	Inject.	350 @ 4,600	375 @ 6,200

Likewise, Power steering is found on most Sting Rays because its front suspension makes it pretty much like a truck at low speed. The limited slip differential isn't included in the base price either, but it is necessary if you're specifying anything but the 250-Powerglide.

☐ By the time you add $81 for real leather upholstery on the bucket seats you're equipped the car in a manner equivalent to the basic XKE with the exception of center-lock wheels and premium tires. You can't get wire wheels from the Chevy factory, but a set of light alloy knock-off disc wheels lists for $322.80. Nylon tires are $16 more, and they compare reasonably with the Dunlops fitted to the XKE. (If you just want whitewalls, they're $32). Tinted glass, power windows, radio, air conditioning, transistorized ignition and such are filligree which don't really count in the analysis.

☐ So, here's the financial picture:

☐ *Jaguar XKE Coupe* with painted wire wheels, bumper guards and seat belts....................$5,700

☐ *Sting Ray Coupe* with 4-speed, L-84 engine, power brakes and steering, limited slip, leather, nylon tires, knock-off wheels....................$5,649

☐ If you want to drop back a notch on the engine option, the Corvette can list for $5,241. And if you want to extract all the prestige which goes with an XKE you'll have to take the chromed wheels and that means, $5,875.

☐ Is a $5,241 Sting Ray competitive with a $5,700 XKE in performance?

☐ Yes, but just.

☐ The cars are extremely closely matched in acceleration, (both attaining approximately 94 mph at the end of a standing quarter mile) and, unless pushed to the limit of their capabilities by talented drivers will run nose to tail over nearly any road. Finally, however, in top speed the Jag will show a slight superiority and it actually takes the injected Sting Ray to beat one. With the L-84 engine though, there is a noticeable difference and the Corvette emerges better on the basis of lots of horsepower applicable at all times.

☐ Two cars, however, could hardly be more evenly matched in appeal and purpose. What are the features which can lead the buyer to select one or the other?

DESIGN & EXECUTION

■ The biggest thing Corvette has going for it is packaged into: tremendous reliability; parts and service obtainable in any city, hamlet or village and domestic origin. Its biggest drawback is strictly one of aesthetics . . . not necessarily in external appearance, (which is a matter of taste and appeal ROAD TEST does not presume to pass on) but in the subtle lack of elegance in design and execution. This is a hard matter to define, but simply stated it is the invisible factor which causes night club parking lot attendants to put E Jags in the front row and stick Sting Rays in any convenient hole.

☐ This difference in design concept is apparent throughout both cars. It is the difference in suspension control arms which are forgings or stampings; rack and pinion or recirculating ball steering gear; polished cast aluminum cam covers or drawn steel; genuine wood rimmed steering wheel or an almost undectable imitation thereof. Understand, this is not necessarily a brief for the "classic" method of accomplishing things, but merely to point out how the two cars can get the same job done in different ways . . . with either great approval or virulent disapproval from

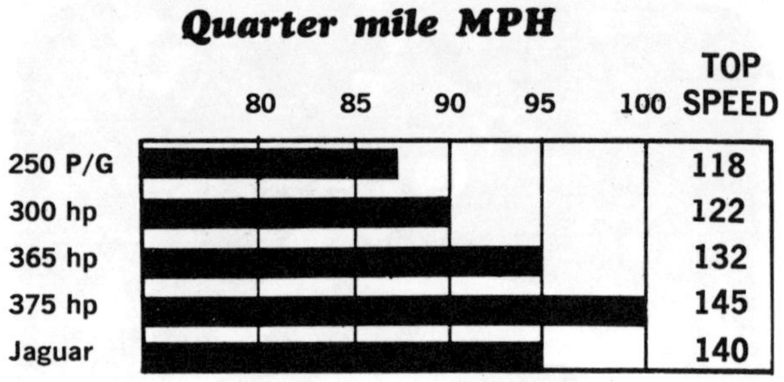

critics on both sides. The manufacturing attitude which spawns the Corvette is one which has made our automobile industry a giant: Design something; build it; sell it; when it goes wrong in service, change it to make it work; build the change into the next model.

☐ With the Jaguar it is: Design something as nearly right as possible; build it; if some one buys it who can't accommodate himself to the design, let him buy something else; if something goes wrong, it shouldn't have because the design was right.

☐ These two attitudes can explain why the S.U. Carburetor and fuel pump are still in production in England and why fuel injection is almost a stock item here.

☐ Jaguar's greatest attribute is that it is a sum of these very factors which are by-passed in America. Factors which make it, in its way, a superb car to own and drive: Handling, performance, execution of design. On the negative side are: gaps in the service chain; a reputation for touchiness in tuning and the well known fact that many minor parts have the lasting quality of cobwebs.

EXTERIOR & INTERIOR SIZE

■ In a side-by-side comparison the cars' differences and similarities are accentuated. They are within 1/16 inch of being identical in overall length, although the Corvette's wheelbase is two inches greater. It is also wider, by four inches and two inches higher. Body lines make it appear much blockier than the Jag and there is actually more interior room in the Sting Ray. The seat-to-roof dimension in the Corvette coupe is two inches greater than the Jag coupe. Another 1½ inches in headroom can be gained by picking the Corvette convertible-hardtop, but you'll lose an inch in the equivalent Jag. Effective headroom is improved in the Sting Ray by virtue of the fact that the seats are raked back 28°. The Jag's buckets are more nearly vertical and in the new 4.2 model, are more padded than before, bringing passengers closer to the instrument panel.

☐ Neither car has provisions for other than two passengers although small children, or an uncomplaining adult, can be carried in the nominal luggage space of the coupe. The Jag coupe comes off better here, more luggage can be stowed and is more easily accessible than the Sting Ray because of its rear deck door. The XKE roadster is less well blessed. Its capacity is strictly limited, whereas the Corvette roadster has ample room for a touring twosome's luggage.

CREATURE COMFORTS

■ Because of the intrusion of the transmission tunnel neither of these cars will win any awards for stretch out room. It is completely non-existent on the driver's side and

HOW THEY COMPARE

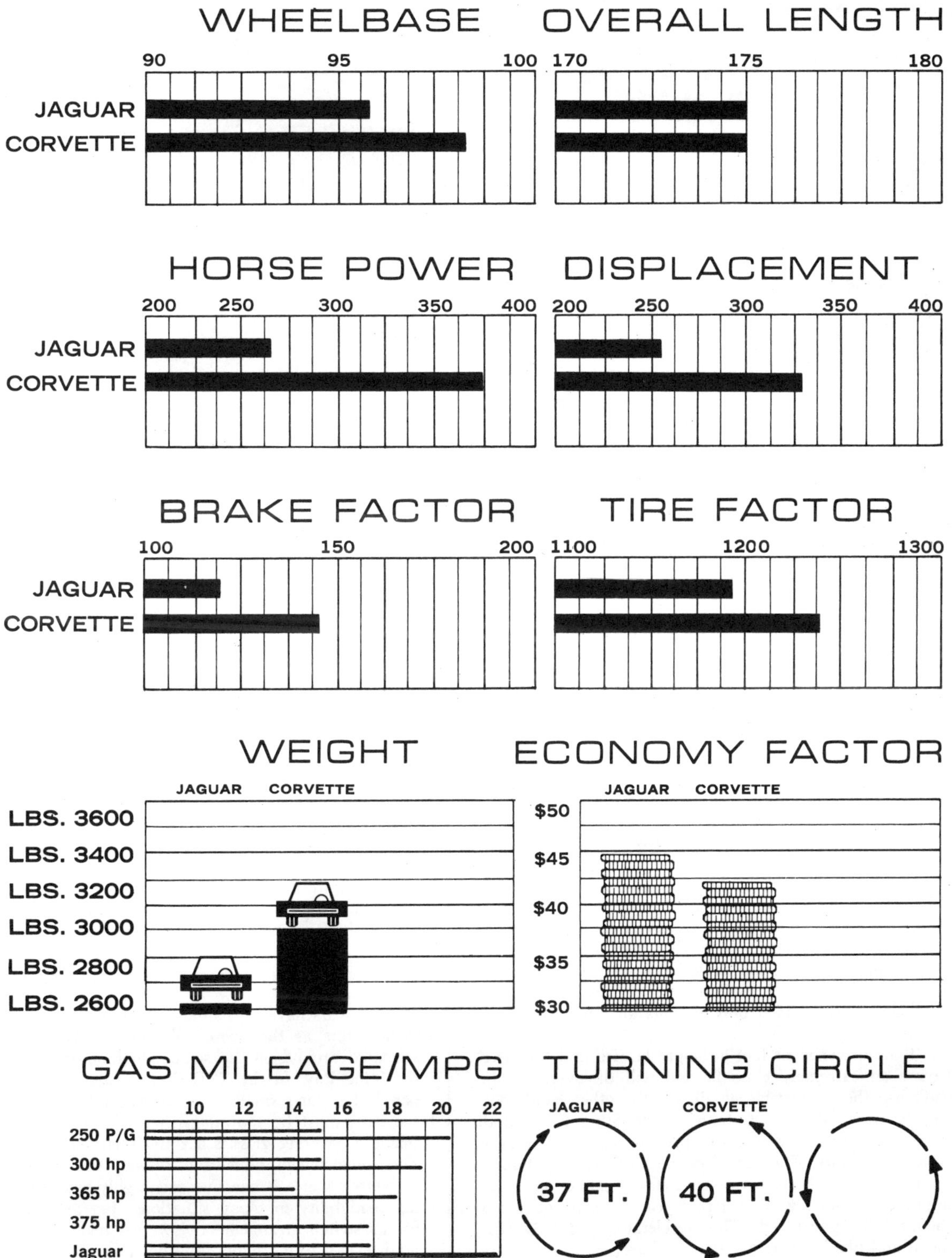

• Six-foot driver's head touches roof of Jaguar coupe, there is less headroom in convertible. Wheel position permits slightly more arm extension than Corvette.

• Six foot driver has ample headroom in Corvette, right leg can be extended farther than in Jag. Tunnel makes both cars inadequate in stretch-out room.

WHAT IS AN XKE?

XKE is the designation of Jaguar's sports-touring model. It is available in two body styles: fastback coupe and convertible. A removable plastic hardtop is an option for the convertible. Other options are given in the text.

WHAT IS A STING RAY?

Sting Ray is the designation of Chevrolet's Corvette sports-touring car. It is available in two body styles: fastback coupe and convertible. Either the folding soft top or a removable plastic hard top is standard with the convertible.

---

the necessity for assuming one position with the throttle leg is apt to become annoying to some people. ROAD TEST's Editor, who drove a Corvette some 4,000 miles through Mexico and Central America competing in the *Rally Centro America*, says that, "you either find this position to your liking or you forget it." Being short in stature is not the answer. As many 5′8″ drivers objected as did their taller brothers. If either car had a hand throttle, it would help by allowing the driver to straighten his leg from time to time.

☐ For the short haul, bucket seats are equally comfortable in the two cars, although seating position is noticeably different. Over long distances, however, the more relaxed posture of the Corvette is better but there is some lack of thigh support for the tall driver. Jag seats can be made to recline a bit more by cutting the seat back bracket. The small flip-stop provided only permits an infinitesimal adjustment.

☐ If the driver is six feet in height he will find the XKE Coupe an extremely close fit and will discover that he can't use the convertible at all. On the other hand, 6′2″ can be acceptably comfortable in the Sting Rays. Both adjustable steering wheels are helpful. The Corvette's is easier to operate. The Jag's lets the arms extend more.

☐ Jaguar's pedals are narrow and close together, although improved in this regard over past years, but are obviously thoughtfully positioned. The accelerator pedal is bare metal and tilts back, rather than forward, as in other cars. This is a comfortable angle for the foot and heeling-and-toeing for braking and gear changing is a natural action. The Sting Ray is also well laid out.

☐ The Corvette's heating and ventilating system is typical of the American car; it works and is oversize. Kickpanel vents admit great quantities of fresh air and it is blower-exhausted through roof pillar vents. The XKE does not come off so well. Jaguar is still trying to fit an inadequate Smiths unit into a contrived system and there isn't enough fresh air at the critical lower leg level. The swing-open rear quarter windows create enough negative pressure to make a draft through the car but the tunnel radiates considerable heat. On a typical summer day in Southern California, the Corvette is more comfortable.

INSTRUMENTS & CONTROLS

■ Both cars have big, almost oversize, speedometers and tachometers as the center of interest. Other gages are scattered around on the same panel before the driver in the Sting Ray. In the XKE they are lined up in a center panel. The Jag's small dials are easier to read, (although the eyes must be moved farther), by virtue of the fact that the covering glass is flat and relatively non-reflective. For some incomprehensible reason, the glass over the Corvette's gages is concave and highly reflective, destroying readability in many situations. Jag also gains points for its switch arrangement, low fuel level and low brake fluid level warning lights. Another Jaguar plus is the headlight flasher which activates high beams, whether or not

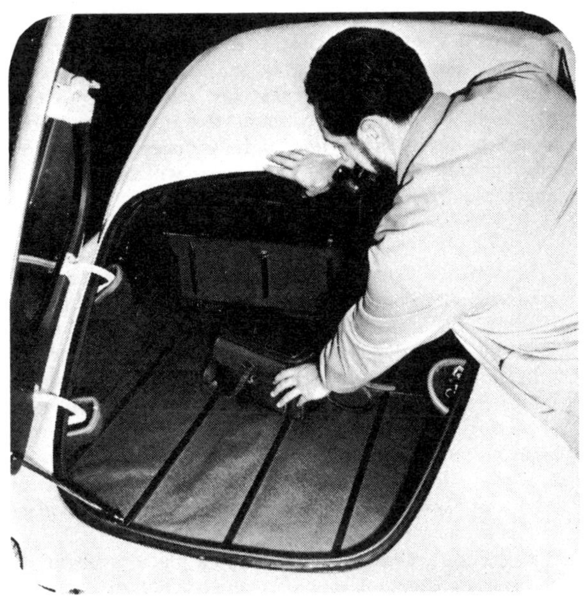

• Luggage space is good in XKE coupe, access is via large rear deck opening. Barrier keeps small objects out of passenger compartment.

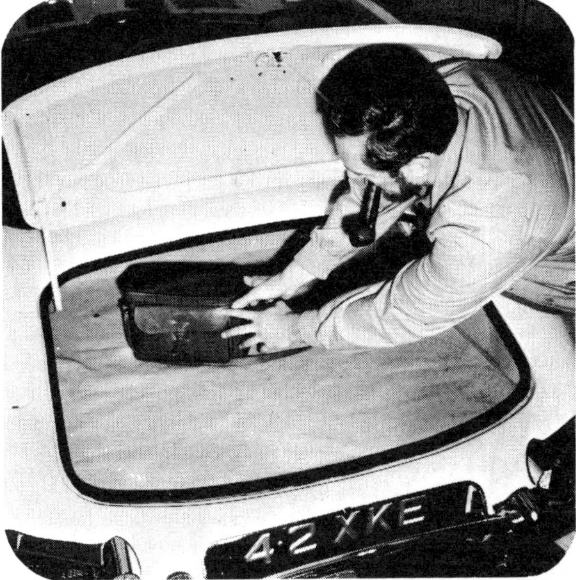

• Carrying capacity of Jag. convertible is minimal. Spare tire is under floor in both cars. Corvette's spare is easier to remove and replace.

the lights are on, enabling you to signal another driver of your intention to pass without honking the horn. The headlight-dipper is on the instrument panel. Some drivers prefer the conventional foot switch of the Corvette.

☐ Instrument location and readability is about all that Jag has going for it in this department however. The Smiths instruments, notably tach and speedo, are highly unrealiable and one can safely predict a short, happy life for them. The problem is in the tiny gears and components plus the fact that there is no oiling wick and the future owner is at the mercy of whatever young lady assembled the gage as to whether it was properly oiled in the first place. On the other hand, Corvette's Delco stuff has gears somewhat like those found in washing machines and they can be lubricated in service.

POWER TRAIN

■ Jaquar's new 4.2 engine (258.4 cubic inches) is a still bigger bore version of the same six cylinder double overhead cam powerplant which has been in service since 1949. Approximately 100 more horsepower is being wrung out of this engine than in its original form and, while it is not overstressed, it works pretty hard. (The bhp rating is fairly accurate, incidentally.) Oil consumption (500 miles per quart) is considerably greater than most American car owners expect and the average XKE owner has some sort of complaint about carburetion or ignition problems at some time. The S.U. carburetors are of a unique variable-venturi type which is more time-consuming to adjust and synchronize than the more conventional fixed-venturi type. Highly-dyed, gummy gasoline, lots of cold running on short trips and lack of attention causes them to give more trouble than, say, the Carter or Holley on the Corvette. Pinging, sooting and breaking down of plugs are common complaints, generally caused by too much use of the choke, excess spark advance or too lean a mixture favored by most mechanics. However, some blame can be placed on the advance curve in the distributor itself which does not permit enough retard at low engine speeds which drivers are prone to use simply because the engine pulls the car uncomplainingly.

☐ The XK engine has a good record for longevity but in pre-1965 models the Lucas starter and generator required replacement long before those in the cheapest American car. This year an alternator has supplanted the generator and a constant-mesh starter has finally done away with the antiquated Bendix drive which rammed gears together at each time the button was pressed. The electric fuel pump was submerged in the fuel tank in earlier models and gave no trouble in comparison with the S.U. found in so many British models. It has now been moved out into the open and remains to be proven in this situation.

☐ An important thing for the Jag owner is to find a good mechanic and take the car to him regularly. The mechanic won't be as easy to locate as a good Chevy man. The average Jag mechanic will be more intelligent and creative but he will also lack the simple virtue of trusting factory specifications implicitly, which is what is needed.

☐ Jaguar's new all-synchro gearbox is much smoother than earlier models, has a shorter throw to third (preventing knuckle-banging on the instrument panel) but is still full of whine. Jags have little transmission or rear end trouble but when problems occur, they're more expensive to repair than Chevrolets.

☐ The old reliable 327 V8 in the Corvette isn't as glamorous or as handsome as the XK, but it seldom gives any static and has good power . . . not as much as advertised, unfortunately. The 375 bhp comes closest to living up to its press notices, but the others are rated about 20% too high. The art of tuning the fuel injectors isn't as widely practiced as the less sophistigated carburetion systems, but procedure is spelled out in the shop manual available to every dealer and the unit seldom goes bad except from inexpert tinkering.

☐ Corvette's four speed gearbox is extremely smooth, quiet and rugged. Provision is made for an adjustment on the shift lever to make the throw shorter or longer, a nice touch, but either way it is accurate and easy. Powerglide, while strong and willing, is only a two-speed and loses some performance for this reason. Like the Jag, few troubles here, but when they come, parts and services are at hand.

THE CARS IN USE

■ There is quite a difference in the road feel of the two cars, although they are the same size. The Jag definitely feels smaller and more like an extension of the driver. A principal factor is rack and pinion steering, which, regardless of ratio, gives a more definite feel of the road than any other type. There is almost no play at the steering wheel in dead ahead position, so a slight movement makes something happen up front. The Jag's shorter turning circle also contributes. In handling, they are equally matched although one seems to work a little harder in pushing the Corvette to maximum. In brakes, the nod must go to Corvette because of reserve. The XKE has just enough brakes, no more. They're great, smooth and precise but on the edge. Corvette's discs surprise every new driver with controllability. They'll go as far as tires will permit.

□ Both cars have a considerable amount of freeway hop, with the Corvette being worse than the Jag. (Some stretches of old concrete with tar strips every 20 feet will rattle your brains in a Corvette.) Ride otherwise is about even (speaking of the stock suspension in Corvette . . . the optional HD suspension is for racing). Noise level is slightly higher in the Sting Ray coupe whose plastic body amplifies more than the Jag's metal shell. Again, wire spoke wheels seem to transmit less road noise than solid discs, so this may enter into it. The main drone sound from the XKE is exhaust resonance.

□ Windshield wipers and washers on the Jag are far superior to the Corvette, but, like all the rest of its genuine rubber components, the blades don't last very long. Jag weatherstripping, moldings and so on soon disintegrate unless carefully maintained with a rubber dressing. The Sting Ray uses neoprene which is more impervious to weather. The small vent-return tube in the gas tank of the XKE succumbs within the first thousand miles and the car smells strongly of fuel until it is replaced with plastic. The chances are that the distributor drive dog at the back of the cam will shear pretty early, maybe before the instrument gives up. Turn signal switches are quite apt to stop operating in the first year and if the car is left in hot sun daily, the imitation leather will begin to peel off windshield posts and dash. If the owner operates at factory-recommended tire pressures and only motors gently, tires will wear in the center of the tread too soon. If he drives pretty hard, fine. If he reduces the pressure about 4 pounds ride will be good, wear will be good, but he can't play Dan Gurney on corners.

SUMMARY

□ The top two Corvettes are a good match for the XKE in performance, comfort, convenience, handling, braking and safety. They are better suited to the person of above average height and require relatively less maintenance to remain in good operating condition. Parts and services are easier to find in most areas and more reasonable in cost than the Jag. As Jaguar's current ads say, "This isn't a car you can buy and forget. . . " It requires attention to details. But, with such attention, the automobile will present an elegant appearance long after the Corvette's fiberglass body has become a little frowzy.

□ You can forget list price, except as a place to begin, on both cars. In times of plentiful supply, Jag dealers will give $400 to $500 off list on the $6,000 piece. Corvette dealers will do even better if you catch the right one at the right time. On resale, you're going to take quite a depreciation, period. At this point in time the year-old, non-injected model will fetch something over $3,000 wholesale. Jags have been about $200 to $100 back of book for nearly a year, so around $4,000 might be expected. Unlike Corvette people, Jaguar owners seem to keep their cars for longer than the two-year period which is the normal trade in period for many buyers because of basic satisfaction and lack of model change. This helps the depreciation factor since the curve flattens out with time. If you are the meticulous type you can have a cream puff Jag several years from now and recover pretty well. If you are a person who buys a car to drive and not to play with, better take the Corvette. There isn't anything on the market to compare with the fairly-stripped, 350 hp, 4-speed Corvette which lists at $4,660 and it must be considered a best buy in this category. However if you want the good things you'll have to escalate to about $5,500 on a deal and then you get into the coin-flip area.

□ ROAD TEST rates the FI Corvette and XKE as equal values and feels that the determining factor is strictly one of buyer personality.

• Jaguar instruments stretched across panel are more readable than Corvette's under-hood grouping.

CARS ON TEST

MET-OFFICE MOTORING

E TYPE JAGUAR 4.2

A HIGH PRESSURE BELT IN A 4.2 litre E Type Jaguar

WHEN YOU PAUSE TO THINK, if this is an activity which appeals to you, that the Jaguar concern is one of the young men in the British motor industry it comes as a bit of a shock to realise for how long the name has been synonymous with real high-performance motoring. In recent years the XK series has always been well out in front of the currently quickest machinery, and for the past two or three years the "E"-type has carried the flag in no mean manner.

Good as it was, the 3·8-litre model wasn't ideal in several ways. Its worst single feature was a gearbox with a built-in crunch and a slow, heavy change, while the seats and general interior finish didn't show up all that well either. The brakes tended to be a bit uncertain at times, too, and that was not a reassuring thought at the speeds of which the car was capable.

Six months ago, however, Jaguars brought out the 4·2-litre version which we can safely say is just about as big an improvement as it is possible to achieve. The "E"-type now is rapidly approaching the happy state of perfection, and if this isn't surprising in view of the experience Jaguars have had in ultra-high performance motoring, it has certainly made the latest model into a car which must be one of the most satisfying cars in the world to drive.

The car we had on test was the fixed-head coupe, a small boy's dream of a car with a smooth but mean and determined appearance, staggering performance and impeccable road manners. It is not, perhaps, the easiest car in the world to get into and out of, especially if the girl-friend is trying it in a tight skirt, but it is a car which has to be put on like a pair of trousers. Once you're in, it fits you like a glove, if this remarkable mixture of metaphors doesn't stop you staying with us. The seats are a vast improvement on the earlier ones and now give full support where full support is needed. You shuffle it backwards and forwards until the pedals are the right distance away, and then you do the same with the adjustable steering column until you are settled and comfy, looking either like Jim Clark or Tazio Nuvolari according to taste.

And then you look round. Slap in front of you are two big, easily-read dials, one reading to 6,000 r.p.m. and the other to 160 m.p.h.: a driver with a heavy boot will see the needles of both of them using all that matters of the dials. Over in the middle of the facia are an ammeter, fuel gauge, oil pressure and water temperature gauges above a row of switches for lights, panel and interior lights, heater fan, ignition, starter, map light, two-speed screen wipers and electric washers, with, on the right-hand side, a warning light for loss of brake fluid/handbrake "on" and a dipswitch. Looking over the wooden steering wheel you see out over one of the most imposing bonnets since vintage days—a great long sleek

affair, with a colossal power bulge in the middle which may cut off some of the view when you're going up a steep hill—but hell, it's worth it. You can aim the "E"-type like a gun. Start her up, then. You switch on first and then push the button, just like the good old days, and if she's warm she'll fire straight away. If the engine's cold, you'll need a bit of choke and, unlike all other models in the Jaguar range, this is something you'll have to do yourself. Nothing to pull, though—just slide a lever up and down a slot. Full choke is needed only for a few minutes, even in cold weather, and after that you slide the lever down again to the position marked "Run" and the motor will do just that, without any spitting or banging about. Actually, "our" car had a stiff and sticking choke control, which meant that we had to leap out, open the bonnet and wriggle a hand down between two of the carburettors to fiddle—and also to lose a good deal of skin off the aforesaid hand.

Two of the carburettors? The "E"-type has three S.U.s, each big enough to keep goldfish in. The engine itself is still a six-cylinder, of imperial dimensions and a bore and stroke of 92·07 mm. × 106 mm. to give a total of 4,235 c.c. It is not, in fact, just a bored-out 3·8 but is virtually a new engine, the cylinders having been re-positioned in the block (to permit the larger bore) and thus using a new, stiffer seven-bearing crankshaft, with a torsional damper. The stroke is unchanged

JAGUAR E TYPE 4.

Engine: Six-cylinder, 92·07 mm. × 106 mm. (4,235 c.c.); c 1; triple S.U. H.D.8 carburettors; O.H.C.; 265 b.h.p. at
Transmission: Diaphram spring clutch, four-speed and synchromesh on all forward gears and central, floor mou
Suspension: Front, independent with coil springs, wish Rear, independent with coil springs, tranverse links and
Brakes: Front, 11 in. dia discs; Rear, 10 in. dia. dis assistance.
Dimensions: Overall length, 14 ft. 7¼ ins; overall wid height 4 ft.; turning circle 37 ft.; kerb weight 22½ cwt.
M.P.H. per 1,000 r.p.m. in top gear—24·5.

PERFORMANCE		
Maximum Speed—see text		
		m.p.h.
SPEEDS IN GEARS	First	— 50
	Second	— 80
	Third	—110
		secs.
Standing quarter-mile		15·25

ACCELERATI

from the 3·8, but the new bores have been fitted with (obviously) pistons of a new type. Maximum power i 265 b.h.p., as on the smaller (well, everything's relative) er but the peak is reached at a slightly lower engine speec there is noticeably more urge in the middle speed range

Right then, the motor's warm. If you'll allow your left to fall off the steering wheel, you'll find that it drops r on to a gearlever, and when this happens you can pok into first. You'll manage it, too: a new baulk-ring syn mesh gearbox has synchro on all the forward gears, an days of try, try, try again for bottom gear when the c standing still are gone. The clutch is a diaphragm-s pattern which made its appearance in the later 3·8 "E"-t it is precise, requires what might be described as med weight pedal pressure and does not slip. Not that there be any need to try, because the improved low-speed pe mance of the engine means that there is plenty of power about 1,500 r.p.m. upwards.

Handbrake off, and you're off. You might well be drivin of the fastest cars on the road, but at this stage you'd guess it. The "E"-type's traffic manners are perfect, and can bumble through the town with the best of the pre "eights". You can, if you fancy the idea, trickle along at a 1,200 r.p.m. in top, which is about 28 m.p.h. Light stee which needs only about 2½ turns from lock to lock, lets swing the great car about almost as nimbly as a Mini with a great deal more satisfaction. The engine is sweet flexible and, if you can tear yourself away from it for enough, you could safely let Auntie borrow it for shoppi it certainly wouldn't bite her.

And now it's hey for the open road—or at least for passes for it in this busy little island we call home. Act the road is seldom open enough for the "E"-type, or else never crowded, depending on how you look at it. If you bombing along at a nice steady 130 or more for hour hour, then I'm afraid you'll just have to go some place but acceleration which will take you from rest to very n 130 m.p.h. in about half-a-minute, plus brakes which r stop you, means that pretty well no gap is too small, and can get places all right if you want to.

Meanwhile, back at the ranch, what are we doing? we've just slotted it down into third and, with the right

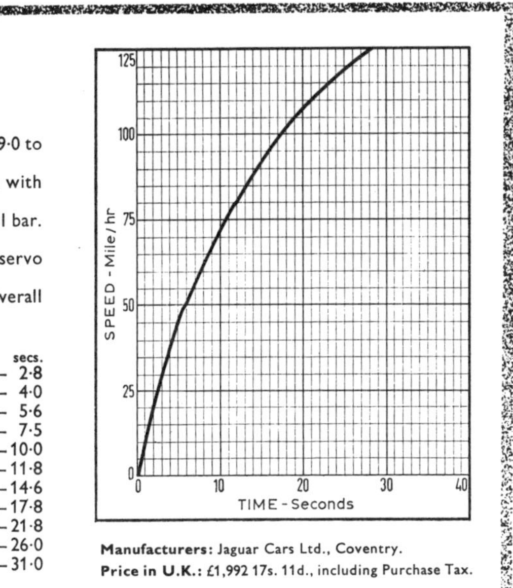

Manufacturers: Jaguar Cars Ltd., Coventry.
Price in U.K.: £1,992 17s. 11d., including Purchase Tax.

ly down, we are waiting for the revs to build up. There t long to wait. Here she comes, 5,400 on the clock and ady we are doing the ton or more. Into top now, which ps the revs to about 4,200, and we're fairly swinging along 00 m.p.h., a speed the "E"-type will keep up all day and night too if necessary.

'll hold it there—this road is one of the curvy ones. The '-type's suspension—all independent, of course, with wish- es and torsion bars at the front, tubular links, radius arms twin coil springs at the back—keeps her going where she's nted. Luckily it's open country, we can see what's going despite the bends in the road, and we can enjoy this bit. t bends—just point her. Slower ones? Well, like we said, ything's relative. Slot it down to third, apply the right hard and she'll go round, balanced beautifully and nout fuss.

ually, during the test we encountered a good deal more n was strictly reasonable of ice, snow and other wintry leasantness, but at no time did we find outselves em- rassed by anything the "E"-type did. Under all these umstances it performed in as well-mannered a fashion as d on decent surfaces, and in fact cornering on ice at fairly n speed was so enjoyable that we wanted to go and do it in. With about 40 lb. in all four tyres, icy surfaces induce rtain amount of understeer, which is so easily balanced by cious application of power that the whole manoeuvre can executed in the most flattering fashion: the car slides as as you want it to and no further, even at high speed und 80 m.p.h. or so) and although we tended to confine sort of exercise to deserted dual carriageways in the early rs of the morning, in fact the amount of leeway could be nicely judged that the white line down the middle remained rossed. So, for that matter, did the driver.

this is greatly helped by nice positive steering, light enough oth low and high speeds and needing only 2½ turns from to lock. At motorway speeds, which can go up to 130 es an hour and more provided you don't keep the needle he red for too long, you don't so much steer the car as the wrists, which is the way it ought to be. Of course, at t sort of lick the motorway is not only pretty short but it lso rather crowded, and even momentary inattention can vide you with a pretty successful accident. Thus it is nice to know that the car will stop, and a new type of servo com- bines with Dunlop discs on all four wheels (inboard at the back, and with separate hydraulic circuits to front and rear) carries out the duty very smoothly. In this connection we must add some very high praise to the 6·40×15 Dunlop RS5 tyres, which provide outstanding grip in a straight line as well as guarding against the dreaded side-slip: on one occasion we confess that we were caught out when, in pouring rain well after dark, we wrongly concluded that a pair of dim specks which glowed red in the murk ahead were the rear-lights of a car about half a mile away. In fact, they turned out to be the dying glow-worms fitted to a car of pre-war vintage, inadequately maintained and certainly largely ineffective: the immediate point, however, was that he was only about 200 yards ahead and travelling at about one-third of our 100 m.p.h. speed. With no room to pass for the moment, the situation could have been tense, but firm application of the anchors slowed the car withous fuss or drama—even on that worst possible surface—thanks to excellent help from the tyres. A long story, perhaps, but well worth pointing out as an "unsolicited testimonial".

At all speeds the massive but discreet power unit—the car is a lot quieter than it used to be—has a pleasantly unburstable feeling, and the new crankshaft serves if anything to improve the already spectacular smoothness of the Jaguar "six".

Jaguars ask you politely not to maintain it at over 5,000 revs for long periods—they naturally have nothing against it in short doses—but this is not all that much of a hardship. On the 3·31 axle which is fitted as standard to all cars except those destined for Italy, France, Belgium, Germany and Holland, which have a 3·07 ratio, and U.S.A., Canada and Newfoundland, which have a 3·54 axle to provide really startling acceleration as some compensation for the legal inability to accept high speeds, 5,000 r.p.m. corresponds to about 120 m.p.h. in top, just over 90 in third and about 65 in second. You can, of course, wind it up further than this in the gears, and in fact at 5,500 r.p.m. you are doing speeds of 50, 80 and 110 in first, second and third cogs respectively.

The suspension and riding comfort, you'll find, are virtually identical with those of the 3·8-litre car except where you find a man-sized portion of extra comfort from the new seats. For those who insist on knowing, the front end has transverse wishbones and torsion bars controlled by telescopic dampers, with a stout anti-roll bar, while at the back there is full independence by means of a lower transverse tubular link, pivoted at the wheel carrier and at the subframe, adjacent to the diff.; this, combined with the half-shaft universally-jointed at both ends, locates the wheel laterally. Fore-and-aft location is provided by the sub-frame itself and also by a radius arm, while dual coil springs, co-axial with telescopic dampers, provide the suspension medium. It is, in fact, a very smooth ride. There is very little roll on corners and in fact the whole thing stays fairly level all the time, no matter what is happening to it. Bad surfaces can be really rushed over before body movement becomes very pronounced, although if it does, watch your head: the roof is a bit low, and one of our tame six-footers found contact occasionally. Directional stability is good—you can take your hands off the wheel at well over the ton without drama—and side-winds don't have any disastrous effects. At the same time the car is far from dead, and if it starts thinking about sliding you get plenty of warning, in good time to do something about it.

Now then, what else? The luggage space: you can stuff suitcases into the coupe by means of the opening rear panel,

which is hinged at the side and can only be released from inside the car by means of a rather fiddly catch behind the driver's seat. Bulk is less important than height here: there is a large floor area, but if you start piling things on top of each

Shades of the Riley Imp and M.P.H.-Tripplewipers.

other you will lose all your view behind you. The rear window is pretty large, but it is also fairly horizontal, and in any case makes the image in the mirror somewhat distorted. "Our" car had the optional electrically-heated rear window which, in the bad weather we suffered, was as near indispensable as makes no difference. All that weather, incidentally, meant that we made heavier than usual use of the electrical accessories such as the rear window, the heater, the screen wipers, the lights, and so forth, but the alternator, which reaches maximum charge at only slightly above tickover speed, dealt with the demands admirably. A Good Thing—if you have an "E"-type in the drive it hurts more than usual if you have to push-start it! But we had no trouble in this respect.

The actual performance of the car is certainly startling in terms of sheer "figures". Checking ours, we find that the acceleration is nearly enough the same as that of the 3·8—in other words, from a standing start you need 7½ seconds to reach 60 m.p.h., 11·8 to get to 80 and the 100 comes up in 17·8 seconds. For what it is worth you can reach 120 m.p.h. and then come back to rest in the mighty half-minute, more or less, and it takes only 31 seconds to get to 130 m.p.h. But the "E"-type, as we have said before, is a gentleman of a car, and while any car which will rush about like this is impressive, for those on board at the time there is nothing in the least savage about the process. One minute you're there, the next you've gone, and to disappear up the road like a stage magician through his cupboard does not necessarily involve either wheelspin or high revs before take-off. The ultimate maximum speed, too, is similar to that of the 3·8-litre car: when we tested that, some eighteen months ago, we actually got 151·2 m.p.h. in one direction, but this took us the odd rev or two over the top. The 4·2-litre model, equally, will do a genuine 150 m.p.h. in both directions, and that, friends, ain't hanging about.

If you drive the "E"-type at moderate speeds, and use the acceleration merely to keep up with other traffic, you will get about 20 m.p.g.—perhaps a little more, but not much, because the "E"-type's low-drag shape helps it to use little more juice at high speeds than it does at low. If you thrash it about the countryside, using the pleasant new gearbox to the full and indulging in three-figure speeds where possible—and the acceleration makes them possible in a lot of strange places—you'll find that it gets through a gallon of petrol in about seventeen miles. And we can think of a lot of two-seaters that won't get within three seconds of the Jaguar's 0-60 time, nor within 30 m.p.h. of its maximum speeds, which don't do better than that.

Almost the only snag about the "E"-type is the insurance companies, who have not yet caught on to the fact that just because a car is fast, it is not necessarily dangerous. The "E"-type, in the right hands, is easily one of the safest cars on the road—largely because of, not in spite of, its performance, and it is certainly less likely to contribute to a traffic jam than most!

JOHN BOLSTER TRIES DICK PROTHEROE'S JAGUARS

I RECENTLY spent a splendid weekend at Husbands Bosworth which included a delightful party *chez* Dick Protheroe. The subject of this short article, however, is the driving of Jaguars rather than the consumption of champers.

The first machine I tried, just to play myself in, was a 2.4 with a moderate tune-up and twin SU carburetters. This had been owned by a client who had recently traded it in, and it had done a large mileage in modified form. The Jaguar 2.4 was a pleasant car, but it tended to be under-powered. This one was altogether different and I timed it at just over 109 m.p.h., which, as a matter of interest to other 2.4 owners, is indicated as 120 plus on the speedometer dial. To give a new lease of life to a very good but rather dull car, this conversion can be recommended.

After a pleasant run with Dick in his Mk. 10—which is in perfect tune and runs as sweetly as you would expect—I took over his XK 120. This open two-seater looks perfectly standard, having even the big vee screen, but the new wire wheels and high-speed tyres give the game away. Actually, a lot of work has been done, rack and pinion steering having been fitted, which has necessitated the use of the inclined radiator instead of the earlier vertical one. Stiffer springs, both front and rear, and a really hefty anti-roll bar are featured, the brakes, of course, being discs.

Yet the car retains the almost vintage appearance of an original XK 120 and, being highly polished, it causes a lot of interest when parked. The engine is a good 3.4, not excessively tuned but set up about right. This car handles impeccably, being as different from an early production Jaguar as it could possibly be. It feels taut and can be slid through bends under perfect control. Without an overdrive, one has to watch out for over-revving on top gear, but on winding roads it would take a very good E-type to keep this old warrior in sight.

My final Jaguar was the famous competition coupé which has been carrying the Protheroe colours in international events. This is an E-type with a fixed-head body which gives remarkably low drag. The engine is a 3.8-litre with fuel injection and the car was exactly as it had been in the 1,000 km. race at Montlhéry when I tried it. A five-speed gearbox is sometimes used, but for this race a four-speed close-ratio box was fitted, simply on the score of weight-saving, the ZF all-synchromesh device being quite remarkably heavy.

After thoroughly warming up the car, Dick had a go at the standing quarter-mile, which caused the clutch to smell somewhat, but a time of 12.8 secs. was recorded. This shows just how much faster a race-tuned machine is than a standard model, and accounts for the success of the Protheroe coupé. Geared for the Montlhéry road circuit, the car was giving about 150 m.p.h. at 6,000 r.p.m. and the very high bottom gear was not ideal for standing start acceleration figures.

When I took over, Dick suggested that I should slow right down to 20 m.p.h. and then put my foot on the accelerator in top gear. With fuel injection, this resulted in remarkably rapid acceleration straight up to 150 m.p.h., when I eased my foot to avoid over-revving. I decided that 6,000 r.p.m. was enough for a "guest conductor", though the owner pleads guilty to having touched 6,700 r.p.m. Of course, with a Le Mans final drive ratio, much higher speeds would be possible.

At 150 m.p.h. the Jaguar was rock steady, needing no holding. At lower speeds on country roads, the hard damper settings could be felt, and one had consciously to keep the vehicle straight over bumps, which is fairly typical of competition cars. In spite of being tuned purely for speed, the engine is entirely flexible and will stand any amount of idling without oiling up or wetting its plugs.

The roadholding of the all-independent E-type is noted for its excellence. Dick Protheroe has done an enormous amount of work on the brakes, and they will now stand any punishment.

I was greatly honoured to be allowed to use this car on the road, for it is not normally put at the mercy of weekend drivers in their little tin boxes, travelling in the safety of its own transporter to race meetings. This vehicle is all fitted up with every conceivable spare part, including a complete rear end already set up with an alternative final drive ratio. All the same, this Jaguar makes a road car of extreme potency with remarkably good manners, which I shall remember driving for a long time.

PROUD OWNER Dick Protheroe poses by his well-known competition Jaguar E-type (top). FUEL INJECTION has been fitted to the 3.8-litre engine, which makes for quite a useful performance (below).

TWO YEARS WITH THE JAGUAR E-TYPE

LAST month, and again this month, we have published letters from a reader, giving experiences with E-type Jaguars, both 3.8-litre fixed-head coupé models. I was particularly interested in these letters as I have just completed two years of E-type motoring myself, with a 4.2-litre fixed-head coupé. This car is used for home and continental motoring in the course of reporting on race meetings for MOTOR SPORT, and other activities connected with keeping the monthly pages filled. I suppose I should refer to my Jaguar 4.2-litre as a staff car, except that when I do it seems to upset a lot of people who had the chance of working for our magazine in the early days, but could not see much future in it; also, nobody else drives the car so it really is for personal use rather than staff use.

It was delivered brand-new, in Carmen red with black interior, the day before the practice took place for the Race of Champions at Brands Hatch in March 1965 and its first trip was to that motor race. It celebrated its second anniversary by taking me to Brands Hatch again for practice for the 1967 Race of Champions, by which time the odometer had clicked round to 71,776 kilometres (approx. 44,000 miles) and I had learnt a great deal about Jaguars and high-speed motoring.

The two readers whose letters we published both seem pretty satisfied with their 3.8-litre cars, but I was never very keen on that model. When it first appeared it looked terrific and I felt I wanted one, but when a Road Test car came along and I tried it I changed my mind. I liked the performance and I liked the steering, but I could not tolerate that awful old lorry-like gearbox and I thought the seats were pathetic. At the time I was Porsche motoring and the E-type felt a great dead lump of a car in comparison and I lost interest. When the 4.2-litre version was announced I renewed my interest, for it had a new all-synchromesh gearbox and new seats apart from numerous other improvements. This time when I borrowed the Road Test car from the Editor I was sold on the E-type fixed-head coupé and decided that it was what I wanted, so I turned my back on ten years of Porsche motoring and moved into a different world, a world of effortless high speed touring in the grand manner. The specification of my car was to suit my special needs, so it was left hand drive as 80% of my fast motoring is in Europe and I do want to see where I'm going when travelling fast. Motoring in Britain consists of short sharp bursts of speed, mostly overtaking slow moving vehicles and I find left hand drive very reasonable. The English stick in the middle of the road by nature, so I can look past them on the nearside before overtaking, and sitting on the left allows you to overtake using the minimum width of road, which is better for everyone. I had a 3.07 to 1 rear axle, which allows 100 m.p.h. at 3,800 r.p.m. and 8:1 compression pistons, instead of the normal 9:1 pistons, so that I could motor anywhere in Europe without worrying about petrol standards. I chose the red colour as I think all fast cars should stand out vividly, and red does this better than anything. It never blends with the background when travelling fast, so people see it coming and move over. The black interior was an obvious choice, me being rather oily and grubby by nature, and I covered the rather thin wood-rim steering wheel with a Romac leather sleeve, tightly bound on and it has proved to be the best 29/6d. worth you could buy. The standard wheel gets very slippery in hot weather and I hate wearing gloves, so this leather rim cover has proved to be the perfect answer. I also settled for a k.p.h. speedo instead of an m.p.h. one as time, distance and average speed running is vital to me in my European travels.

Reader Vose from Vienna suggests that the 1963 Jaguar is the best, but I disagree, for the 1965 cars had numerous improvements. The brake booster system was completely re-designed and is trouble-free compared with the earlier system, the gearbox is an obvious improvement, the electrical system incorporates an alternator instead of an old-fashioned dynamo, and because of the greater output it can support much more powerful headlights and a heated rear window, an item that is not necessary until you've had the use of one. I could not tolerate driving a car with a rear window that continually misted up or got covered in rain, for I do like to know what is going on behind me. He criticizes the arm-rest-cum-box between the seats, but I find this enormously useful and on the 2 + 2 this has been reduced to nearly half the size and it has become almost useless. It sounds as though he has done away with the air filter system for the carburetters on his Coombs-tuned engine, but that is something I would never do on a car being used all day and every day, especially on an E-type for the front wheels throw an awful lot of muck back into the engine compartment, in spite of rubber sealing strips. I fully agree with him that 100 m.p.h. is a good cruising speed for the E-type, and at that speed you can back right off the throttle and average 20 m.p.g. on European petrol, though if reader Lees from County Down is to be believed Irish petrol gives even better results (or is it Leprechaun Juice ?). Fuel consumption depends entirely on how you drive, if you keep the accelerator pedal hard down and accelerate at the maximum and run the engine to 5,000 r.p.m. all the time you will do 16 m.p.g. If you press on pretty effectively an overall 18 m.p.g. is easy to achieve; if you pussy-foot on the power you can do 20 m.p.g. and if you drive it with the performance of an average family bread and butter saloon you can do 22 m.p.g. I've no doubt that if you ambled along at 32 m.p.h. with no perceptible acceleration you could achieve 25-26 m.p.g. While running in for the first 1,200 miles I was getting a constant 22 m.p.g.

John Lees says how he gets a thrill from flooring the accelerator at 100 m.p.h. and seeing the nose come up. This is so true of an E-type and when motoring on Autobahns, Autostrada or Motorways I find I am constantly doing this to avoid obstruction travelling at 60-70 m.p.h. The acceleration from 90 onwards is one of the real charms of the E-type and is my "standard" for the valuation of so-called fast cars, and not many match up to it. This acceleration goes on with a progressive feeling to 135-140 m.p.h. and after that every m.p.h. can be counted, the most I have achieved being 143 m.p.h. by rev-counter reading.

When friends heard that I was getting an E-type they said "A good car, but you will spend all your time picking up little bits that will fall off." They were quite wrong, as were those who said everything but the engine would wear out. As regards the engine they were right, in 40,000 miles it has had routine oil changes, routine (10,000 miles) plug changes, new points at the same time on principle rather than necessity, routine oil filter changes and the top timing chain adjusted twice and is still going like a bird. Oil consumption in the first 10,000 miles was appalling, but after that things settled down and now it is just heavy but reasonable. Jaguar are still working on this problem, but they never seem to do anything in a rush at Coventry. For the first 10,000 miles the gearbox was "all right" but nothing to rave about, but after that it improved noticeably and is now a joy. The movement was stiff and notchy to start with but as it became "run-in" it loosened up nicely and from experience I can say that it is a far better gearbox when you are using it with the right hand from a left driving position, the movement being so much nicer. I kept a detailed log of the mileage I covered and by 10,000 miles nothing had happened apart from the original RS5 Dunlop tyres being completely bald and the front brakes pad non-existent. I had followed the routine service instructions thoroughly, doing the work myself as I don't trust the average garage mechanic, and the only fault that had arisen was that the indicator flasher light on the instrument panel failed, though the flashers themselves were still in order. At 20,000 miles still nothing had gone wrong or fallen off, but the rear axle started growling at about 15,000 miles. I was about to set off on a trip to Italy and the noise sounded as if I would not get to the coast, let alone Italy, but there was no time to worry so I just motored on. Other Jaguar owners consoled me by saying the back end was built like the Forth Bridge and it would not break, and the noise was pinion bearings. By the time I got back I was so used to the noise, and as it had settled down and was consistent, I ignored it and at 40,000 it was no worse, but while having a new clutch fitted I had the axle unit replaced as a precautionary measure, at that mileage.

I had given the car a trouble-free target of 10,000 miles, which it achieved easily, and at 20,000 miles nothing had broken, fallen off or let me down, but for the next 10,000 miles I suffered the way my friends told me I would suffer in the first 10,000 miles. The dirt and rust of ages got at one of the front disc brake calipers and it went on and stayed on, which meant stripping the whole unit, then the alternator/water pump driving belt gave up from old age and broke, and one of the motor-cycle type silencers under the tail fell off (old age and bad design). I welded it back on and stiffened the mounting, but then the other one broke, so I threw them both away and made up a straight-through pair of tail pipes which are slightly noisier but not obtrusive and they will not fall off. The nylon driving dog for the electric rev-counter motor wore out and though a new one cost only 1s. labour costs to replace it would have cost £2 10s !. An expensive fault was at 25,000 miles when the alternator voltage regulator burnt out and with 30 amps being churned out the battery knelt down and quietly died, which left me stranded for a few hours until parts could be found in Milan. Then the Calabrian mountain roads broke the right hand bonnet catch, which involved more welding, since when the bonnet has never fitted quite as nicely. At 36,000 miles I motored too rapidly over some undulating Austrian roads and wrote off one of the exhaust down pipes from the manifold, these being very vulnerable and I did it again on an English road at 43,000 miles. This is partly due to using lower profile tyres than the original Dunlops, so Jaguar cannot be blamed, but ground clearance is a bad point on the E-type if you are like me and drive in a rough and unruly manner on undulating roads. At 38,500 miles an expensive trouble intervened when the alternator packed up, the diodes having burnt out, and a new A.C. alternator is no simple financial problem like an exchange dynamo, but such is the march of progress and you have to pay for improvements. In spite of the cost I would not think of returning to the old-fashioned D.C. dynamo system with its limited output, for with the alternator you can have 200 watts of light shining forwards, wipers, heater fan, heated rear window, fuel pumps, ignition, clock, instrument lights and radio all working at once and the battery is still kept charged. As Monte Carlo Rally competitors have often found, a load like this just creases the average D.C. dynamo. Having just got over this problem I suddenly ran out of brakes and this was the first serious fault to arise, with the mileage at 39,000 miles. Fortunately it was on a slow 2nd gear corner and I was able to scrabble round without an accident. A rubber piston in the brake system slave cylinder developed a tiny score mark, which let the fluid past and I was without any front brakes and back brakes only are pretty ineffective, especially as mine by this time were getting oily from a rear axle seal that was leaking, so as 40,000 miles came up I decided it was time for a pretty thorough overhaul, in preparation for another 40,000 miles of hard use. The front brake discs by this time were rather like corrugated iron and the suspension ball joints were a bit loose and rattly and the clutch, though working perfectly, was obviously going to wear out soon, for like the brakes, if you really use an E-type, it does a lot of work dealing with over 250 b.h.p.

It may seem as though I have had endless troubles but really it has been more a question of maintaining the ravages of hard usage and a rough life. My E-type does not spend much time shut up in a heated garage, nor does it do any quiet commuting or any town driving, it lives in the mud and roughness of the country and is used consistently for long and short journeys and is used well, being afforded nothing in the way of pampering other than a sympathetic mechanical ear and a mechanical " feel " to the driving. When this article is taken down to the village to post it the E-type will take me there at a highly illegal speed, and even faster on the way back, there being strict times and places to achieve 4,000 r.p.m. in top gear, but as reader Vose says, it will be in the " safety category " at all times, for it has such vast reserves if used as a fast touring car. For one short 10-mile dash, on the Targa Florio circuit, I tried using it as a GT car, reducing the reserves to a minimum. I kept the engine at 5,000 r.p.m. by really using the gearbox, used the brakes and acceleration to the full, and cornered over the limit of the Goodyear tyres. It was very exciting *but very dangerous*, and convinced me that the E-type in standard form is not a GT car; if you use it as a T car for Touring in the Grand Manner it is very nice indeed and well ahead of a lot of GT cars anyway. It is a safe car providing you do not provoke it, unlike cars such as the Porsche 911, the GT 40 Ford, a Lotus Elan or the new Dino Fiat, for they revel in being provoked and seem to say " come on, have a go, it'll be all right, we'll stay with you." The E-type seems to say " watch it chum, don't do anything unruly that might embarrass me."

Tyres, like oil, plugs or petrol are mostly a matter of personal choice and after many experiments I am happily motoring on Goodyear G800 radial-ply tyres, with 30 lb./sq. in. in the front ones and 35 lb./sq. in. in the back ones. An E-type on equal pressures front and rear is a rather dangerous joke, no matter what make of tyre. I put Autolite plugs in the engine and just forgot about them until a routine renewal was due, and I pour Castrol oil in the engine by the quart and fill the tank with any Super grade petrol, from the most expensive Esso to cut-price unknown brands and " free-gift " Total petrol. However, I must disagree with Mr. Vose on the tank capacity of a nominal 14 gallons being adequate, especially on inter-continental trips and 17 gallons would have been ideal. The reserve warning light is first-class; mine starts flashing after 267 miles from a full tank, and I run completely dry after 330 miles, so you have 60 miles of warning of low fuel level. I find that you can have peace of mind all the while the orange light goes out under hard acceleration in second gear and the remaining fuel surges to the back of the tank; when it stops doing this you really must look for a petrol station.

If there is one complaint I have about Jaguar in general it is the way their agents seem to be letting the side down. I don't expect to get spare parts over the counter in foreign countries, but I do expect it in England, just as I don't expect to get everything for a VW or Porsche in this country, but I do expect it in Germany. Oddly enough I seem to be able to get *everything* for my various Volkswagen machinery at my local agent, whereas my local Jaguar agent is just a joke. It has a very famous name and poor Mike Hawthorn would turn in his grave if he could read this. It is not as though I ask for rare and complicated bits, far from it, but it would be quicker and easier for me to drive up to Coventry and visit the works. Another Jaguar agent with famous racing associations, in Guildford, was no better, the storeman happily telling me the part number of the bit I wanted and adding " but we haven't got one." When I got on to Henly's main depot in London, who are well stocked, it proved to be the wrong part number anyway ! A Jaguar agent in Malvern gave the impression of never having heard of an alternator, while another in Barnstaple had every sort of driving belt for the alternator apart from one for an E-type. However, they were very helpful and made a jury-rig that got me to Plymouth where Pike & Co. Ltd. were 100% efficient and everything that a Jaguar agent should be. The thought of having the car serviced and maintained by the average agent would make me lose interest in the car, for it would spend most of its time sitting in the workshops waiting for the inefficiency of the stores to catch up. The sort of things that I consider let the side down are the first exhaust down-pipe that was produced from the stores that was so rusty that I refused to accept it; the second was reasonable but the welding was cracked, but as it was all that was available I took it and re-welded it myself. Later I did not bother to try and get a pipe, it was quicker to get the hacksaw and welding plant out and make my own exhaust system. When a slight error of judgement broke the plastic side-light/indicator lens the local stores took a week to produce a new one, which was delivered, but the following week another one was delivered ! Too much or not enough seems to be the motto for service.

Like our two readers Messrs. Vose and Lees I am a very satisfied Jaguar user and will probably stick to E-types until we have enough readers to justify the expense of a Ford GT 40, Ferrari GTB, or Lamborghini Miura. Having got used to 250 b.h.p. and real acceleration at high speed in an effortless manner, coupled with a docility with which Auntie could cope, I would be reluctant to motor in anything less than a 4.2-litre E-type, which means that I shall stick to the very satisfactory way of life that is MOTOR SPORT and race reporting.—D. S. J.

JAGUAR E-TYPE 2+2

Road test of a 138 mph four-seater

WITH the splendid opulence of many fine pre-war cars the Jaguar E-type always seems to occupy a lot of road space in relation to its two-seat passenger capacity, but the new two-plus-two coupé added to the range in April is much more a car for the family man than the egotist. To answer generally the many specific questions put to us while testing the new model, it will certainly seat two adults and two children, say up to ten years old, in comfort—for an outlay of £2284 the owner has a family sports car capable of close on 140 mph, still with the remarkably good comfort and handling that has made the " E " so successful.

It is powered by the 4.2-litre version of Jaguar's famous six-cylinder, twin overhead camshaft XK-E engine developing 265 gross and our test car was equipped with a new option, Borg Warner 8 three-speed automatic transmission and a torque converter. With this form of drive the " E " feels more like a very fast saloon than a sports car, for despite the speed it is extremely quiet and smooth.

Essentially the styling of the E-type is powerful and beautiful but the upright angles of the windscreen pillars strike a jarring note and this is accentuated in the 2 + 2 by the roofline which is two inches higher. Need has rightly overcome aesthetics, though, because headroom is ample for four occupants and obviously the most important thing about a car is that it should be comfortable. Offsetting the greater height the wheelbase and overall length have been increased by nine inches and the doors are wider to give easier access; the width remains unaltered, but the floor has been lowered to improve footroom.

Performance and handling

Taking into account an extra three hundredweight on the kerb weight, slightly greater frontal area and the extra power absorption of the automatic transmission, it was surprising to find that the maximum speed is 138 mph, only about 14 mph less than that of the two-seat E-type with four-speed transmission. So far as Britain is concerned top speeds are fairly academic at the moment, but the 2 + 2 can, with 2.88 final drive, cruise almost indefinitely at 120-130 mph keeping just below the red sector on the rev-counter; at maximum speed the engine simply runs out of power at 5300 rpm.

Maintaining a cruising speed of about 120 mph on a motorway in hot weather brings the temperature gauge up to a steady 80 deg C, about the point where the electric cooling fan cuts in, rising to 90 deg in town traffic. A 200-mile journey at these speeds brought the fuel consumption down to 17 mpg, but the return trip showed some improvements—cruising at around 100-110 mph in the evening the 2 + 2 returned a creditable 19 mpg, and the water temperature stayed around 75 deg C. Oil pressure maintained a steady 45 pounds all day.

If the enthusiast wanted full performance as well as load-carrying capacity he would probably choose manual transmission and save £140; we know from experience that the new all-synchromesh four speed box is a vast improvement. As a touring car *par excellence* the automatic version is splendidly restful and easy to drive though lacking the last ounce of performance; for instance in D 1, giving the range of three gears, it took 21.5 seconds to reach 100 mph compared with about 17.5 seconds for the manual-change two seater. We did not find it satisfactory to use the hold low because there was an appreciable lag between moving the lever and the actual change, so unless the change was anticipated the engine could be damaged. The upward change anyway was jerky and sometimes the box went straight to top gear. Our times therefore were taken with D 1 selected, which is the way most owners will drive.

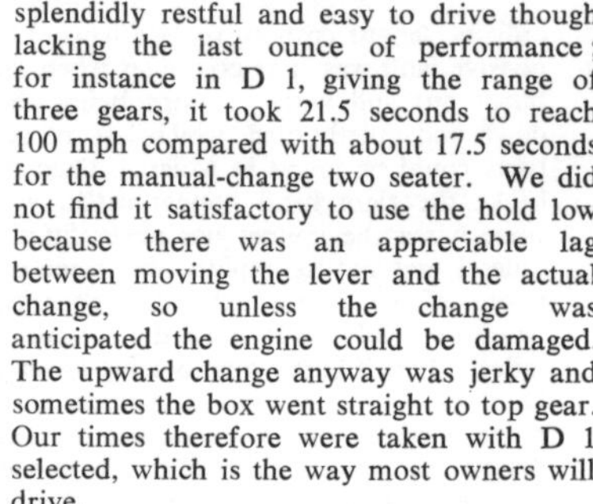

Hold low is useful all the same, because slipping the lever back one notch from D 1 gives an instant and smooth change-down into intermediate for cornering, low being selected automatically and held if the speed drops below 20 mph. Changes up are made at 5000 rpm (55 mph) and 4800 rpm (87 mph), but holding intermediate will take the E-type comfortably beyond 90 mph.

The most impressive thing about the performance is the remoteness of the engine. More effective heat shields have been fitted to the bulkhead to isolate the engine heat from the interior and the overall effect is to practically eliminate engine noise until the unit approaches 5000 rpm. All one hears is a deep and muffled booming from the dual exhaust system, maintaining a constant pitch as the car accelerates and the torque converter steadies the engine speed.

The suspension is surprisingly soft for a sports car, though it did not bottom at speed on undulating roads when three adults were aboard. In fact the 2 + 2 gives a really comfortable ride coupled with outstanding handling characteristics. There is no sign that the increased length has upset the handling in any way, the car having almost neutral steering characteristics throughout the speed range, finally oversteering just enough to give one the confidence that a tightening bend can be dealt with easily. When breakaway point is reached the car moves slowly with plenty of warning and remains very easy to control. A limited slip differential puts all the power on to the road around tight corners and should make a lot of difference on wet roads.

At first the steering seemed to be incredibly light, yet it retained plenty of feel. Exactly half the 27.5 cwt kerb weight is on the front wheels and with a steering ratio giving 2.5 turns from lock to lock one would expect heavy steering at parking speed, but this is certainly not the case. Competition drivers may complain about the rubber mounting of the steering rack but for all normal purposes it gives precise and shock-free control.

Braking from high speed brings to mind the reverse thrust of a jet plane when landing, without the noise. Disc brakes are fitted all round—inboard at the rear—with servo assistance, and all we can really say about them is that they do all that is required of them constantly, smoothly, and with light pressures. Headlights are shielded behind toughened glass fairing which seems to reduce the beam intensity despite more powerful bulbs being fitted. Night-time maximum speeds would not be much more than 90 mph and the dipped beam does not travel very far; a headlight flasher is fitted.

Continued on page 51

AUTOCAR, 12 October 1967

Jaguar E-type

AT A GLANCE: Very refined, powerful, but docile sports car. Smooth, economical and mechanically quiet twin-cam engine with agreeable gearbox. Excellent steering, poor lock, reassuring fade-free brakes. With hood up or hard-top, needs better ventilation. Many detail improvements in design, equipment and finish.

MANUFACTURER
Jaguar Cars Ltd., Browns Lane, Allesley, Coventry.

PRICES

Basic	£1,599	0s	0d
Purchase Tax	£368	3s	2d
Seat belts (ex. fitting)	£8	0s	0d
Total (in GB)	£1,975	3s	2d

EXTRAS (inc. PT)

Chromium plated wire wheels	£52	4s	9d
Radio and aerial	£42	0s	5d
Hardtop	£83	11s	8d

PERFORMANCE SUMMARY

Mean maximum speed	140 m.p.h.
Standing start ¼-mile	15·0sec
0-60 m.p.h.	7·4 sec
30-70 m.p.h. (through gears)	6·5 sec
Fuel consumption	23 m.p.g.
Miles per tankful	320

FRANKLY our drivers all enjoy testing E-types; this is the fifth time since our world first of March, 1961. Previously they have all been coupés—3·8 and 4·2-litre with 2 or 2+2 seating; this time it is a smart yellow 4·2 roadster.

Anyone who compares the several sets of figures may be either surprised at their general consistency or puzzled by small discrepancies. We shall not attempt to analyse them here, but would mention that through the years the weight of the coupé has gone up as more equipment and comfort has been built in; tyres and their rolling radii have changed; the much improved bigger-capacity engine has been developed to give better torque rather than more sheer power and gear ratios have been altered.

To complete the introduction, let it be added that we ran a very early 3·8 roadster as a staff car for over three years and therefore we shall naturally make some comparisons between that and the latest test car.

Exterior appearance has changed scarcely at all in six years but recently the faired-in headlamp covers have been discontinued—probably at a cost of 2-3 m.p.h. of top speed. Maybe this has also slightly improved the headlamps and reduced stray beams, which can be a plague in mist or fog. The lamps are still no better than satisfactory for 70 m.p.h. at night. If you feel inside the radiator slot you will find the top is now single skinned, which will simplify repairs of dents in this vulnerable nose.

Inside the cockpit many improvements have been made. Black reflection-free leather and pvc are used for seats and trim; only the bright steering wheel spokes now dazzle when the sun is high above or behind.

Both seats are better shaped and padded, and are as good as they could be in the rather limited space available. Of course they can now slide farther back, and this, together with little wells in the front floor gives more leg room for a tall driver or passenger. The steering column adjusts for reach and can also be raised or lowered on its supporting links (this is a simple spanner job, the first universal joint being under the instrument panel).

Autocar road test number 2153

Make: Jaguar
Type: E Roadster
4,235 c.c.

TEST CONDITIONS

Weather: Fine dry. Wind: 0-10 m.p.h.
Temperature: 15 deg. C. (60 deg. F.)
Barometer: 29·0 in. Hg.
Humidity: 50 per cent
Surfaces: Dry concrete and asphalt

WEIGHT

Kerb weight: 25·4cwt (2,848lb-1,293kg) (with oil, water and half-full fuel tank)
Distribution, per cent: F, 49·4; R, 50·6
Laden as tested: 29·4cwt (3,289lb-1,493kg)

Test distance 3,149 miles Figures taken at 19,100 miles by our own staff at the Motor Industry Research Association proving ground at Nuneaton.

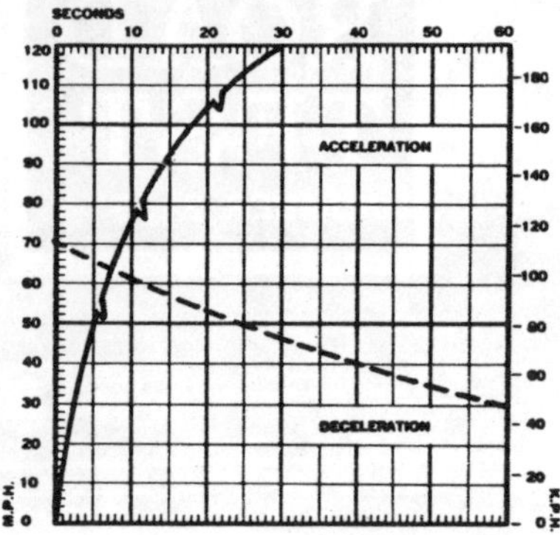

MAXIMUM SPEEDS

Gear	m.p.h.	k.p.h.	r.p.m.
Top (mean) (with hood up)	140	225	5,650
(best)	141	227	5,680
(with hood down) (mean)	130	209	5,240
(best)	131	211	5,280
3rd	112	180	5,750
2nd	82	132	5,750
1st	53	87	5,750

Standing ¼-Mile 15·0sec 89 m.p.h.
Standing Kilometre 30·1sec 120 mp.h.

TIME IN SECONDS	2·9	4·0	5·6	7·4	9·4	12·4	15·1	17·1	23·1	30·1
TRUE SPEED M.P.H.	30	40	50	60	70	80	90	100	110	120
INDICATED SPEED	32	42	51	61	71	82	92	102	113	123

Mileage recorder 6·1 per cent over-reading.

Speed range, gear ratios and time in seconds

m.p.h.	Top (3·07)	3rd (3·90)	2nd (5·34)	1st (2·68)
10— 30	—	—	3·9	2·7
20— 40	—	4·9	3·1	2·2
30— 50	5·2	4·3	3·2	2·5
40— 60	4·7	4·5	3·6	—
50— 70	5·7	5·0	3·8	—
60— 80	6·1	5·0	4·8	—
70— 90	6·2	5·4	—	—
80—100	6·8	6·5	—	—
90—110	7·7	8·9	—	—
100—120	9·0	—	—	—

FUEL CONSUMPTION

K.P.H. 50 60 70 80 90 100 110 120 130 140 150 160
M.P.G. 10 20 30 40 50 60 70
LITRES/100 km 5 6 7 8 10 12 14 16 20
M.P.H. 30 40 50 60 70 80 90 100

(At constant speeds—m.p.g.)

	Top
30 m.p.h.	31·5
40	32·2
50	31·5
60	28·8
70	27·2
80	24·7
90	22·4
100	19·7

Typical m.p.g. 23 (12·3 litres/100km)
Calculated (DIN) m.p.g. 24·7 (11·5 litres/100km)
Overall m.p.g. 21·8 (13·0 litres/100km)
Grade of fuel, Super Premium, 5-star (min 100RM)

OIL CONSUMPTION

Miles per pint (SAE 10W/40) .. 300

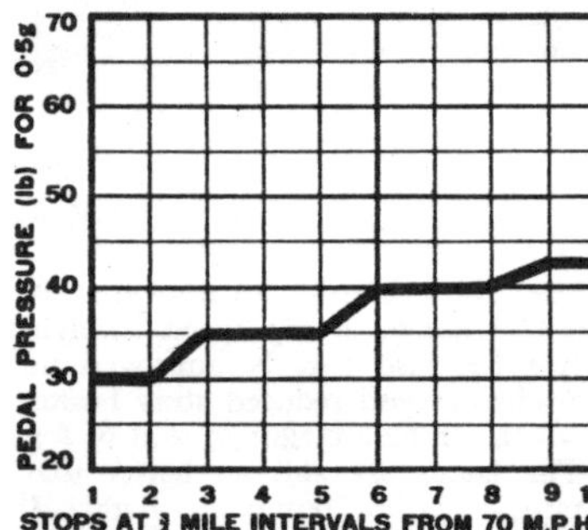

BRAKES (from 30 m.p.h. in neutral)

Load	g	Distance
25 lb	0·37	81 ft
50 „	0·81	37·2 „
60 „	0·97	31·0 „
Handbrake	0·37	81 „

Max. Gradient, 1 in 4

Clutch Pedal: 40lb and 5in.

TURNING CIRCLES

Between kerbs L, 37ft 6in.; R, 39ft 10in.
Between walls L, 39ft 5in.; R, 41ft 5in.
Steering wheel turns, lock to lock .. 2·8

DIPPING MIRROR
TEMPERATURE GAUGE
OIL PRESSURE GAUGE
LAMPS
FUEL GAUGE
AMMETER
GRAB HANDLE
GLOVE BOX
HEATER & DEMISTER
BONNET RELEASE
VENTILATOR
REV COUNTER
INDICATORS TELL-TALE
CLOCK
SPEEDOMETER
IGNITION LIGHT
LOW FUEL LEVEL TELL-TALE
MAIN BEAM TELL-TALE
HANDBRAKE & BRAKE FLUID WARNING LIGHT
DIPSWITCH
INDICATORS & HEADLAMP SIGNALLER
BONNET RELEASE
HORN
CHOKE WARNING LIGHT
CHOKE
VENTILATOR
INTERIOR LIGHT
PANEL LIGHTS
2 SPEED FAN
IGNITION
HANDBRAKE
CIGAR LIGHTER
ASH TRAY
MAP LIGHT
STARTER
SCREENWASH
WIPERS
1 3 R 2 4

HOW THE CAR COMPARES:

MAXIMUM SPEED (mean) M.P.H.

100 110 120 130 140
Jaguar E-type
AC 289
Austin Healey 3000 Mk III
Lotus Elan S.E.
Mercedes-Benz 230 SL

0-60 M.P.H. (sec)

20 10 0
Jaguar E-type
AC 289
Austin Healey 3000 Mk III
Lotus Elan S.E.
Mercedes-Benz 230 SL

STANDING START ¼-MILE (sec.)

30 20 10
Jaguar E-type
AC 289
Austin Healey 3000 Mk III
Lotus Elan S.E.
Mercedes-Benz 230 SL

M.P.G. OVERALL

10 20 30
Jaguar E-type
AC 289
Austin Healey 3000 Mk III
Lotus Elan S.E.
Mercedes-Benz 230 SL

PRICES

Jaguar E-type	£1,967
AC 289	£2,952
Austin Healey 3000 Mk III	£1,126
Lotus Elan S.E.	£1,762
Mercedes-Benz 230 SL	£3,611

There is a better spread of pedals, giving more space between them and a resting point for the left sole off the clutch. The angles of the pedal pads are also more comfortable for human ankle joints.

A central armrest is provided with comfortable sponge-padded top; it forms the lid to a glove box. On the doors are two other armrests which double as door pulls. With safety harness tight, the driver can reach all the levers and switches arranged neatly across the central panel. The two levers which ought to be modified in shape are those controlling heat and air which point dangerously at the passenger.

Plenty of heat comes into the car from the larger matrix now fitted and the two-speed fan is quiet and powerful. Fresh-air ventilation with the hard top fitted is inadequate and it is uncomfortable to open the windows because of the keen draught and wind roar. This car proved almost watertight in heavy rain with the hood up.

A beautiful and accessible engine. Note the bigger, cross-flow radiator and the latest induction manifold with hot water circulation

Steering

The E-type has superbly light and responsive steering to which the radial-ply tyres contribute; the rear suspension and adhesion are also far above average even among the best GT coupés. No car we have tested has had a better balance of handling qualities with high performance for the sweeping corners and rolling hills of British and Continental roads. However after about 1,000 miles the rear dampers became very weak and the back of the car then bounced about, occasionally bottomed and the handling deteriorated. This has been an E-type weakness for too long.

With the exceptional handling and fairly high tyre pressures of 32 p.s.i. minimum all round, goes a relatively soft ride, free of thumps and bumps from suspension and wheels.

If you do not concentrate, you find yourself going into bends 20 m.p.h. faster than usual, such is the deceptive ease of the car's performance. In these circumstances the brakes can be used hard without drama, but it is better, assuming moderate driving skill, if you steer normally and pour on some power as the nose shows signs of running wide, which will bring the car neatly round the bend in a trice.

Since the early models, the braking system has been much improved. It now has a suspended vacuum servo, bigger booster and dual lines. Being power assisted rather than a power system, a servo failure would leave the same braking for a harder push on the pedal. From speeds of over 100 m.p.h. the brakes are spendidly powerful and even, hauling the car back to low speed in an emergency.

If the brakes had not been used for some minutes, as on a motorway, they pulled, usually to the left, on the first application. As the test proceeded—and we drove this car for over 3,000 miles—the pedal movement became long and spongy, needing one pump before response was normal. This was annoying but did not affect the efficiency of the brakes themselves.

The revised system on this 4·2 gives a much better bite at low speeds for an emergency "crash" stop in traffic. Although after hard use the brakes sometimes smell very hot they are virtually fade-free. Now the E type has an effective handbrake which will lock the back wheels and also hold the car on a 1-in-4 gradient, though not quite on 1-in-3.

Several qualities contribute to the car's very high journey speed capabilities. The engine gives a great deal of torque at low r.p.m. and sustains it to peak engine speed, therefore on the Continent momentary checks matter less and the car is back at 100 m.p.h. or over in seconds.

Our figures show that in top gear alone acceleration from 30 m.p.h. to 120 takes under half a minute. On the horizontal mile at the MIRA test track this car comfortably tops 120 m.p.h. from a standing start and brakes easily in time for the tight turn-about loops at the ends. Several standing quarter-miles were timed at 15·0 sec with two up and towing a fifth wheel. The speed at the end was almost 90 m.p.h.

Another reason for high journey speeds is the slick, all-synchronized Jaguar gearbox now fitted. The lever is just by the driver's hand and the movements are light, short and precise. Our only criticism was that the reverse guard spring became very

The boot is shallow but has a big floor area and holds more than one might suppose. The underfloor spare wheel carries a useful toolkit

JAGUAR E-TYPE

weak (like those on the earlier boxes) by the end of the test.

Top speeds in the gears are impressive but are seldom used in practice. Normally we changed up before the start of the red sector on the rev counter. If you take the engine into the red at 5,600 r.p.m. the gears peak at about 53, 82 and 112 m.p.h. On the road 40, 70 and 100 m.p.h. are good working figures to remember.

A third journey quality is the reserve of performance that always seems to be available. A driver can judge just where he wants to place the car in relation to other traffic and put it there almost instantly. Overtaking is decisive and safe. Both occupants are relaxed because the full power can be fed to the road without a moment's worry about wheelspin or twitching the tail round. The Powr-Lok differential does its bit in this respect and in rapid getaways from standstill.

Buying an open car you hope for good weather which we mostly had and the hood was more often down than up. The occupants are well protected in the cockpit and but for a draught round the back of the neck, which a scarf will prevent, you can be warm and snug all day and well into a September night too.

With the shapely hardtop fitted the car is transformed. Engine noises, exhaust roar, rush of wind, all are gone, and in the new quiet you hear some gear whine, maybe for the first time. It is also noticeably less simple to hop in and out. The hardtop is easily attached and allows a better view to the rear, avoiding the blind quarters of the hood. The rubber window sealing strips came unstuck or were rubbed off by shoulders each side but otherwise it proved weatherproof and well insulated. Inside, the enclosed cockpit quickly becomes stuffy and steamed up.

This roadster is faster when the hardtop is on or the hood up. With hardtop (and the normal 3·07-to-1 axle) it will exceed 140 m.p.h.; with hood up it does 140, while open, 130 m.p.h. is its lot. If you fit different tyres, such as Dunlop racing, with a bigger rolling radius to gear the car up, given the space, it will go faster still with the hardtop fitted. We were content to remain standard with tyres as supplied but blown up to 40 p.s.i. (which goes up to 42-44 p.s.i. as they get hot).

Fuel consumption is surprisingly good and despite spirited driving, including very high speeds abroad, the overall figure was almost 22 m.p.g. So the 14-gallon tank gives a comfortable 250 miles between fills on a journey. Constant speed figures show that if, for example, you are trying to save French francs you can cruise on an *autoroute* at 70 m.p.h.

A shapely, snug and easy-to-fit hardtop

Below: More foot and leg room, properly shaped seats, extra safety padding, neater trim and new visors are among the improvements in the latest E-type. The height of the back of the seat cushions can be adjusted

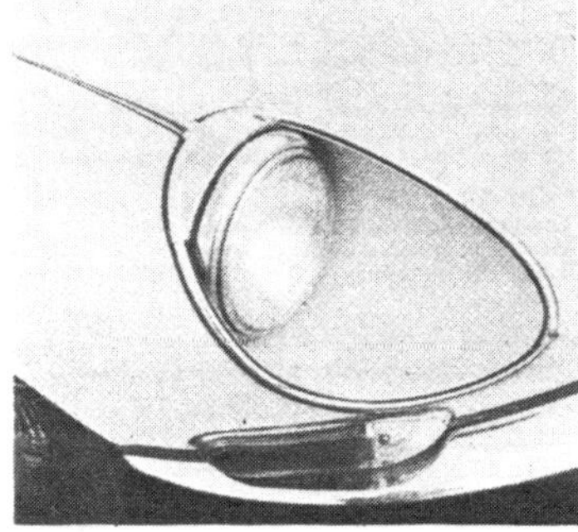

Top: An ideal car for two on tour. The other chap is taking the picture
Above: Headlamps without covers but with new small styling strips over them
Below: In addition to protecting the tail, the bumpers are an essential part of the styling. The boot latch is opened from inside the car. The hood is particularly easy to fold away under its soft cover

(dawdle might be the expression for this car) and expect to get over 25 m.p.g. A light foot and 40 m.p.h. would give at least 30 m.p.g. Of course *autoroutes* as well as petrol are expensive in France. In and out of a city like London, 17 to 18 m.p.g. would be normal. When the reserve warning lamp stops winking and becomes steady there is still between 1 and 1½ gallons left.

Oil consumption, which used to be heavy on some Jaguars was reasonable, working out at 1 pint every 300 miles. One of the improvements for the 4·2-litre engine was to the inlet valve guide seals to reduce oil loss here. The radiator took 3 quarts of water in 3,300 miles.

The engine compartment is a joy. Tidied up and with accessories made more accessible, it remained clean and shining bright throughout the test, bringing "oohs" from those around whenever it was opened abroad. Electrical connections have been getting rather shoddy on cars; a lead fell off the alternator and since, surprisingly, there is no warning light to indicate no-charge, sudden dimming of lamps and fade out of engine were the symptoms of a flat battery. Reconnected, the alternator, which cuts in at just over 700 r.p.m. (running at twice engine speed) quickly had the battery charged up again. Later, another connection fell off the starter solenoid and we had to push-start until we could take a good look underneath to find the fault.

A number of the new safety requirements are already catered for on this E-type and the two universal joints in the steering column make a collapsible section less important. Even so, this extra provision can be incorporated later on without the

JAGUAR E-TYPE

need for other major design changes.

Additional crash padding has been put in around the instrument panel and screen pillars. Measures are ready for cleaning the exhaust to Californian standards on export cars.

Among the minor improvements are better fitting carpets and trim, better doorseals and a tidier under-panel area. An experienced eye will also note the much improved paintwork, and examination from below would reveal more rustproofing and underprotection.

The carrying capacity of the boot is always misleading; it will still hold two quite large suitcases side by side and some extra soft stuff as well. The catch for the lid is inside the car and now has a lock of its own.

If you search through the price list of cars of the world you will find that this Jaguar 4.2-litre roadster is still unique. Its performance, ex-works price, steering, roadholding, tractability, economy, comfort and good looks may be matched by other sports or GT cars but not one of them has the lot. ■

SPECIFICATION: JAGUAR E-TYPE (FRONT ENGINE, REAR-WHEEL DRIVE)

ENGINE

Cylinders	6, in-line
Cooling system	Water; pump, electric fan and thermostat
Bore	92·1mm (3·63in.)
Stroke	106mm (4·17in.)
Displacement	4,235 c.c. (258 cu. in.)
Valve gear	Twin overhead camshafts
Compression ratio	9·0-to-1; Min. octane rating: 100 RM.
Carburettors	3 SU HD8
Fuel pump	SU electric
Oil filter	Tecalemit full-flow, renewable element
Max. power	265 b.h.p. (gross) at 5,400 r.p.m.
Max. torque	283 lb. ft. (gross) at 4,000 r.p.m.

TRANSMISSION

Clutch	Borg and Beck diaphragm spring, 9·5in. dia.
Gearbox	4-speed, all synchromesh
Gear ratios	Top 1·0, Third 1·27, Second 1·74, First 2·68, Reverse 3·07
Final drive	Hypoid bevel with Powr-Lok limited slip differential, 3·07-to-1

CHASSIS and BODY

Construction	Integral steel body with separate front and rear sub-frames

SUSPENSION

Front	Independent, torsion bars, wishbones, anti-roll bar, telescopic dampers
Rear	Independent, twin coil springs and telescopic dampers, wishbones, radius arms, fixed length drive shafts, anti-roll bar

STEERING

Make and type	Alford and Alder rack and pinion
Wheel dia.	16 in.

BRAKES

Make and type	Dunlop disc front and rear
Servo	Lockheed vacuum
Dimensions	F, 11in. dia.; R, 10in. dia.;
Swept area	F, 242 sq. in.; R, 219 sq. in. Total 461 sq. in. (314 sq. in./ton laden)

WHEELS

Type	72-spoke centre-lock wire type, 5in. wide rim
Tyres—make	Dunlop
—type	SP41HR radial-ply tubed
—size	185-15 in.

EQUIPMENT

Battery	12-volt, 60-amp-hr.
Alternator	Lucas 11AC 45-amp.
Headlamps	Lucas sealed beam, 150/120-watt (total)
Reversing lamp	Standard
Electric fuses	8
Screen wipers	Triple blade, 2-speed, self-parking
Screen washer	Standard, electric
Interior heater	Standard, water-valve type
Safety belts	Extra, anchorages built-in
Interior trim	Leather seats, pvc headlining (detachable hardtop)
Floor covering	Carpet over felt
Starting handle	No provision
Jack	Screw scissors
Jacking points	One each side, centrally under sills
Windscreen	Laminated
Underbody protection	Bitumastic on all surfaces exposed to road

MAINTENANCE

Fuel tank	14 Imp. gallons (64 litres)
Cooling system	32 pints (including heater) (18 litres)
Engine sump	15 pints (8·5 litres). SAE 10W/40. Change oil every 3,000 miles; Change filter element every 6,000 miles
Gearbox	2·5 pints SAE 90EP. Change oil every 12,000 miles
Final drive	2·75 pints SAE 90EP. Change oil every 12,000 miles
Grease	13 points every 6,000 miles and 4 points every 12,000 miles
Tyre pressures	F, 32; R, 32 p.s.i. (up to 125 m.p.h.); F, 40; R, 40 p.s.i. (above 125 m.p.h.)

PERFORMANCE DATA

Top gear m.p.h. per 1,000 r.p.m.	24·8
Mean piston speed at max. power	3,760 ft/min
B.h.p. per ton laden	180

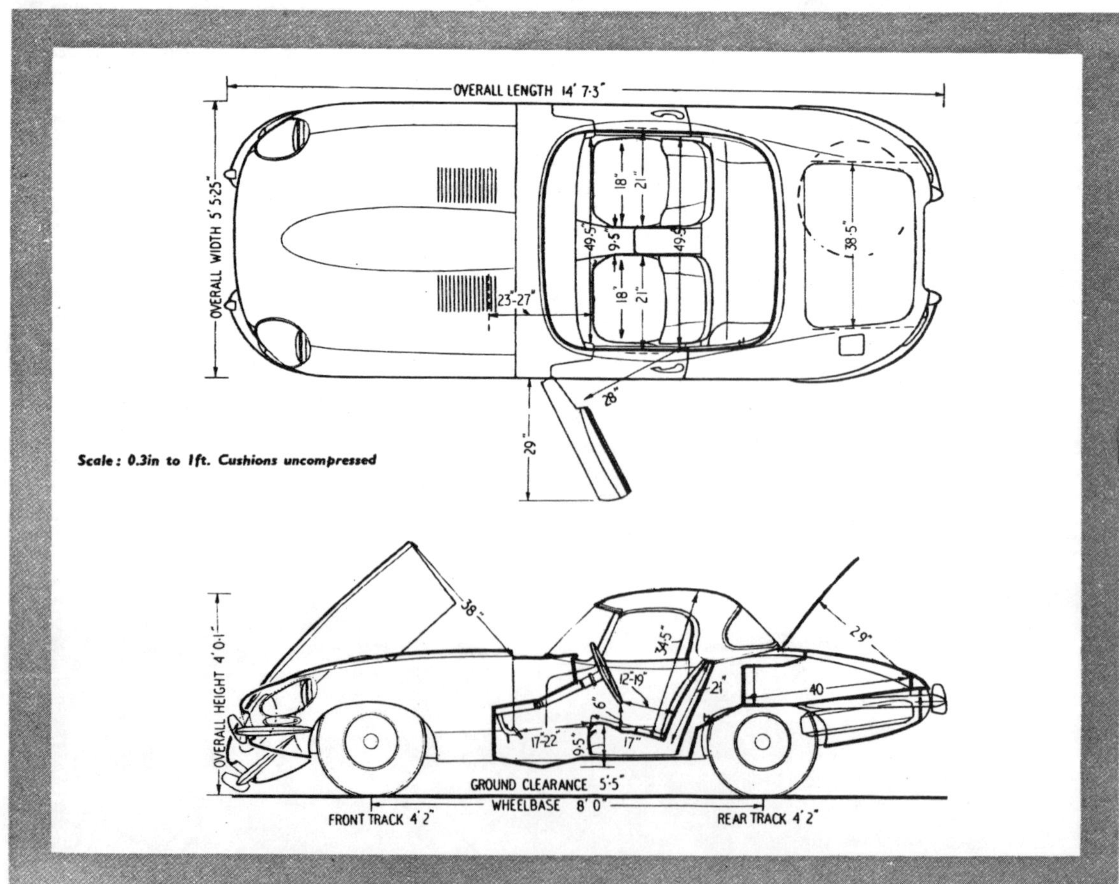

Scale: 0.3in to 1ft. Cushions uncompressed

JAGUAR XK E

$5584
West Coast P.O.E.

First significant changes since addition of 2+2 in 1966, bumpers front and rear are relocated, auxiliary lighting below rather than above bumpers. Twin exhaust pipes separated. Does not obsolete older models. Larger air intake for radiator. Performance and handling above average. Has high eye appeal. Manufactured by Jaguar Cars Ltd., Coventry, England.

Jaguar's 4.2 litre (258.4 cu. in.) twin overhead camshaft six cylinder engine has been with us now for many years. In its latest form, it puts out 246 bhp at 5500 rpm. Twin Zenith-Stromberg carburetors replace the three S.U.'s of the '67 model and are part of the smog device system. The effectiveness of this smog unit can be judged by the emission figures, hydrocarbons 135 ppm whereas the Federal requirements are for 220 ppm. The engine exceeds the intended requirements for California for 1970 by a large margin. The net loss to performance by the reduction in bhp from the three carburetor unit is some 20 horses. In general driving, they are not missed but if you want to show up at the drags, there will be a slight loss when run against the clocks. As the car was never intended as a dragster, it is of academic interest. The other changes on the engine are more interesting. There are now two fan belts, one driving the alternator (from a larger pully thereby getting it cranked up a bit faster) and the other to the water pump. At the rear of the block, there is a better clearance for the water passage which allows the rear cylinder (No. 6) to run a mite cooler. This was the one that gave trouble if the engine ever ran overly hot.

Oil consumption, according to owners, is at last way down on this engine to a mere quart per thousand at the most. This same engine was also in the '68 model so a fair number of miles have been used to testify to this low figure.

The header tank has also been replaced by an expansion tank on the firewall and another bone of contention has been removed. Water hoses and the rubber trim will still require watching as the British still persist in using a high pure rubber content.

When the engine hood is closed down, it is supposed to form a seal around the wheel arches to prevent road muck from being thrown into the engine compartment. This it does not do and dirt and grit get in everywhere. It has been improved some over the older model but is not perfect yet.

The front suspension is independent by parallel wishbones, with torsion bars, telescopic shock absorbers and anti-sway bar. The rear suspen-

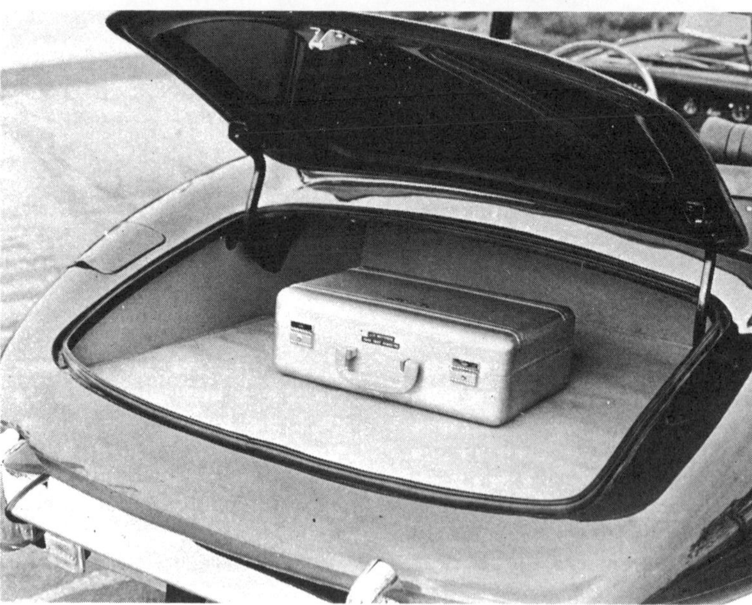

New type safety dash with recessed push-on switches but still the traditional Jaguar layout.

All this space and carpet too? The E-type trunk is surprisingly roomy and vinyl carpet-lined to avoid damage to luggage.

sion unit is a complete assembly and is the most trouble free item on the car. It is fully independent comprising tranverse links, radius arms, quadruple coil springs with four concentric shock absorbers.

The ride is very good for a sports car with this potential and the car will smooth out the freeway joints but not eliminate them completely. Coming out of a corner under power, the rear end sits down well and the car accelerates smoothly and maintains the chosen line without sliding around. On severe braking, the car will dive, naturally, but it is not really that noticeable to the driver.

The use of pure rubber will cause other trouble and the first item to go will be the wiper blades, followed a close second by the rubber trim between the bumpers and the body. Generous use of rubber lubricants is strongly recommended, and by this means, the owner can keep his car looking show-room fresh.

The addition of a 2 plus 2 filled the need for the market that liked the looks of the car and its status appeal yet had outgrown the four on the floor shifting. The automatic version obviously had to come and the extra two seats were a bonus. They are usable by adults in the 5′6″ bracket but whether you can get four people in the car depends on the size of the driver. If he has his seat fully back, you have a three seater. Entry in and out of the four seater is easier due to the larger door (8½″ over the two

ROAD TEST

Supercool! The new Jaguars feature this much-enlarged radiator intake for increased cooling.

Higher bumper, new rear light cluster and back-up lights, new exhaust pipe arrangement. All different for 1969.

seater) although the rear passenger requires a certain amount of agility to enter and exit, and it is something not easily done with grace.

The '69 model 2 plus 2 has had a subtle change in the front of the roof line and the windshield is much more raked giving it better aerodynamics and a bit more room inside. It has smoothed out the humped-back look of the older model. Power assisted steering will be optional for this model in early '69, desirable for the little woman but not necessary for the average male.

The '69s have had a revamp of the instrument panel and the toggle switches have been replaced with the rocker type, all part of the safety requirements. The 'quarter' sized clock that used to be hidden in the tachometer dial has been dumped in favor of a good sized electric type in the center of the instrument panel. This is the same size as the gauges and has even got a fast/slow adjustment screw. From all accounts, it performs well which is more than could be said for the older model, the owner had a 50/50 chance of it working at all.

An extra switch has been added to the panel for the rear window electric heater. This is now mandatory by law but the unit is one that Jaguars have used on their European models for years and is a reliable item. All safety laws have been met and the car now sports an adjustable headrest. The door latches have been recessed and are awkward to operate, there is certainly no possibility of opening one accidentally.

The front and rear of the car have had a face lift and the intake hole has been enlarged to allow better cooling. The turn signal lights at the front and the brake/turn combination at the rear are now below the bumper level. They have been enlarged considerably but as they are not now visible from the side, running lights have been added to meet safety requirements. These tend to detract from what would have been a clean side view of the car. The twin tail pipes have now been separated and the rear bumper position has been raised about 1 ½ ins.

The big change in the '69 car is that the brakes are now Girling discs all around. Previous owners will testify to the eternal squealing that haunted the car for the first 10,000 miles. This could be alleviated by rapid decelerations from speed but was not too practical a solution in many instances. The new discs appear to eliminate this problem but we will

wholesale. Parts are readily available although occasionally there will be shortages caused by the workers going on strike at the factories — an all too frequent occurrence.

All in all, the steady product improvement over the years is at last paying off and the '69 XKE is certainly one of the best to come down the pike in a long time. Its acceptance by the buying public is still high and it is one of the few cars that gets the sophisticated California Freeway drivers to turn their heads and take another look. If it's a toss up between a Jaguar and a Stingray to go on the front line at the restaurant parking lot, the Jaguar makes it a no contest ♠

have to wait a short while for owners' confirmation of this. The brakes are still hydraulically operated with a vacuum servo assist and are quite satisfactory for the little woman to operate without working out at the local 'Y.'

The interior seating is as before and the ventilation system has had minor improvements. They are still not the coolest cars to ride in but the factory is now installing air conditioning which eliminates this problem, albeit at a price tag of $485.00. This is almost $100 less than last year.

Knock off hubs (now require a separate attachment to remove them) are the standard wheel on the car. A mag type wheel will be available early in 1969.

The U.S. market is still the largest one for Jaguars and close to 80% of their entire production comes to these shores. Southern California is by far the largest buyer with upwards of 600 cars being sold in this area alone in a year. If the owner keeps his car for three or four years, he will invariably come out quite well. If he just prefers to add gas and forget it, then come trade in time, he will hurt badly.

In times of plenty Jaguars can be bought for $400 to $500 off on a clean deal. However, 1968 was a lean year for the dealers as regards availability and prices were much firmer. '69 looks like following the same pattern so the market for cream puff used ones should be extremely good. An edgy car will be at least two back of

Jaguar XKE

Data in Brief

DIMENSIONS	
Overall length (in.)	207
Height (in.)	48
Turning diameter (ft.)	37
WEIGHT, TIRES, BRAKES	
Weight (lbs.)	2466
Tires	6.40 x 15
Brakes, front & rear	disc
ENGINE	
Type	6 cylinder DOHC
Displacement (cc)	4200
Horsepower	265
SUSPENSION	
Front	wishbones & torsion bars
Rear	transverse tubular links and coil springs

The price of clean air

How Jaguar faced the American challenge

by Harold Hastings

TWO YEARS AGO Jaguar spent a quarter of a million pounds modifying the E-Type to comply with American safety regulations. New, more stringent regulations have recently necessitated further changes, which are both interesting and expensive, to the Jaguar engine. These are: control of exhaust emission, elimination of breather fumes and prevention of petrol fumes reaching the atmosphere.

Exhaust Emission Control

The duplex manifold system introduced in 1968 to bring the carbon monoxide content down to the permitted maximum level of 1.5 per cent has been made more elaborate to comply with the 1970 level of approximately one per cent. This new level has also involved much closer control of induction temperature to ensure efficient combustion with the leaner air/fuel ratios. The desired result has been achieved by a system that keeps the temperature of the air supply to the carburettors at approximately 120 deg. F.

As the illustrations show, the carburettors receive their supply of air from two sources. Relatively cold air comes through an intake on the end of the air cleaner box. Hot air is drawn from a stainless-steel shroud over the exhaust manifold and passed across the engine by suitable ducting to the inlet of the air cleaner box. This inlet incorporates a plate-type valve arranged so that as the hot-air inlet is opened the cool air supply is restricted and vice versa. This permits a mixture of the hot and cold air streams to give the desired temperature.

These valves are controlled by a pneumatic servo-motor mounted on the inlet of the air-cleaner box and connected by a vacuum pipe to a thermal sensor located on the engine side of the air-cleaner, where it reacts to the temperature of the air entering the carburettors. The sensor controls the depression in the vacuum pipe and thus modifies the intake temperature to the required level. The arrangement is such that, irrespective of air temperature, the hot air supply is shut-off at full throttle when the level of hydro-carbon emissions is not critical. This avoids the reduction in charge weight which would otherwise reduce power output substantially.

In addition to these arrangements, modifications to the carburettors include a new metering-needle form and revised settings for the throttle by-pass valves which control manifold depression during over-run. A further measure against emissions in the critical over-run condition takes the form of a vacuum retard capsule in the distributor which is arranged to retard the ignition by crank degrees whenever the throttle is closed.

Elimination of Breather Fumes

This takes the familiar form of connecting a $\frac{3}{8}$in. diameter tube from the breather housing to the constant depression areas in the carburettors so as to maintain a small depression in the crankcase under all running conditions. In this case, the breather housing is located on the front of the cylinder head and a flame trap and oil separator are incorporated. In addition a further connection is made to the new evaporative emission control—which is the third of the main anti-pollution systems.

Continued on page **57**

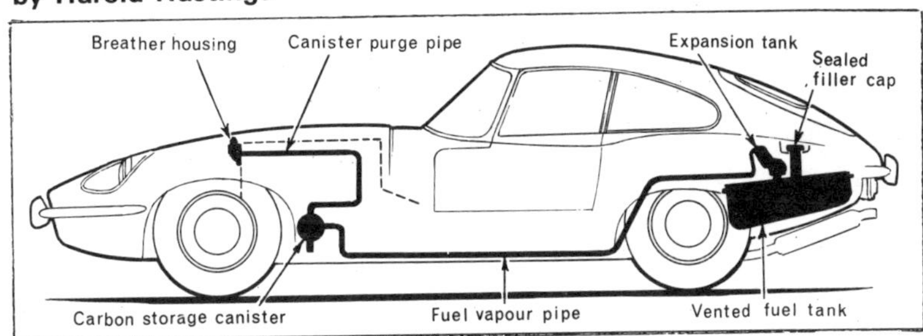

This outline drawing of an E-type shows how vapour from the fuel tank is prevented from reaching the atmosphere. In normal running, it is drawn into the engine and during stationary periods, it is absorbed by a carbon storage canister.

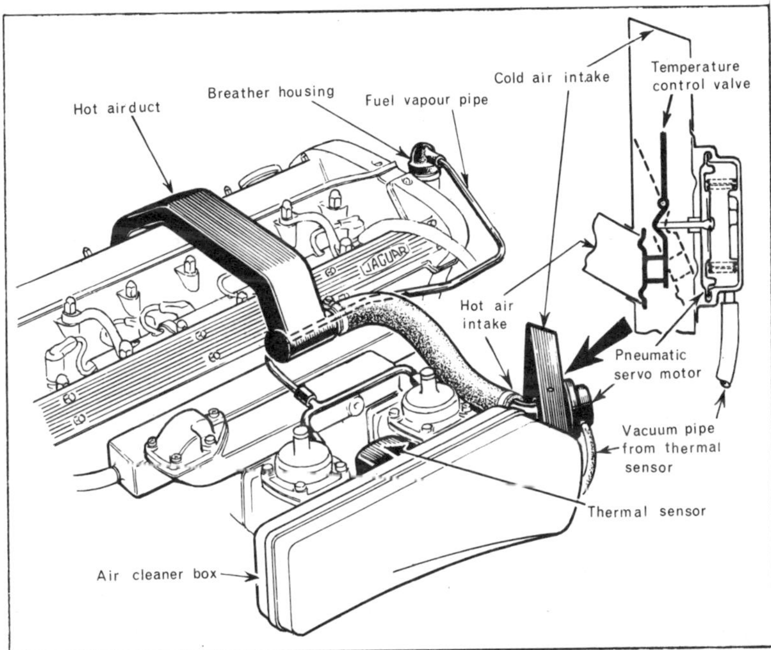

The latest elaboration of the duplex manifold system now used on Jaguar engines below for the US. The drawing above shows the plate-type valve which mixes hot and cold incoming air to give a constant intake temperature of approximately 120 degrees F.

A broken-open drawing of the carbon storage canister used for preventing petrol vapour reaching the atmosphere (see text).

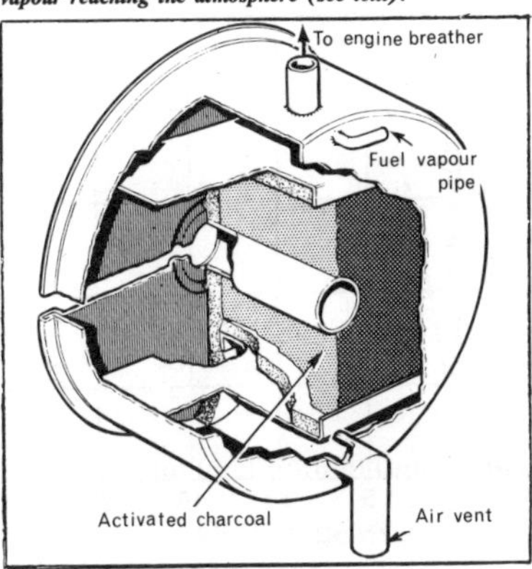

DATA SHEET-JAGUAR E-TYPE

Manufacturer: Jaguar Cars Ltd, UK.
Test car supplied by: British Leyland, Sydney.
Price as tested: $8,389

ENGINE

Water cooled, 6 cylinders in line. Cast iron block, seven main bearings.
Bore x stroke: .... 92.1 x 106 mm
Capacity .... 4235 cc.
Compression .... 9 to 1.
Carburettor .... 3 SU HD8
Fuel pump .... electrical
Fuel tank .... 14 gallons
Fuel recommended .... super
Valve gear .... dohc
Max. power (gross) .. 265 bhp at 5400 rpm
Max. torque .... 283 lb.ft.
Specific power output ...... 62.6 bhp/litre
Electrical system .. 12v, 60 amp hr battery, 45A alternator.

TRANSMISSION

Four speed manual all synchro gearbox; single dry plate clutch.

Gear	Ratio	Mph/1000 Rpm	Max. mph
Rev.	3.085	—	
1st.	2.681	—	50
2nd.	1.739	—	73
3rd.	1.270	—	101
4th.	1.000	23.2	137
5th			

Final drive ratio .... 3.07 to 1

CHASSIS

Wheelbase .... 8ft. 0in.
Track front .... 4ft. 2in.
Track rear .... 4ft. 2 in.
Length .... 14ft. 7in.
Width .... 5ft. 5¼in.
Height .... 4ft. 0in.
Clearance .... 5½in.
Kerb weight .... 26cwt.
Weight dist. front/rear 49.6/50.4 percent
lb/bhp .... 10.6lb.

SUSPENSION

Front: Independent, wishbones, torsion bars, anti-roll bar, telescopic shock absorbers.
Rear: Independent, wishbones with semi-axle as upper arm, trailing lower radius arms, 4 coil springs, 4 telescopic shock absorbers.
Brakes: Front: 10.98 india disc, rear: 10in dia inboard disc, dual circuit, servo-assisted.
Steering .... rack and pinion
Turns lock to lock 2.50
Turning circle .... 41ft.
Wheels: Knock-off wire with centre lock hubs and 185 by 15 tubed radial ply, Dunlop Aquajet/tyres.

PERFORMANCE

Top speed .... 137 mph
Average (both ways) .... 137 mph
Standing quarter mile .... 15.5 sec.

Acceleration

Zero to	Seconds
30 mph	2.7
40 mph	3.9
50 mph	5.6
60 mph	7.6
70 mph	9.7
80 mph	12.5
90 mph	16.0
100 mph	20.5

	3rd	top
20-40 mph	4.4	6.4
30-50	4.2	6.3
40-60	4.1	6.4
50-70	4.5	6.7

BRAKING: Five crash stops from 60 mph

Stop	percent G	pedal
1	.98	53 lb
2	.98	53 lb
3	.95	50 lb
4	.95	50 lb
5	.98	50 lb

Consumption; 21.2 mpg over 950 miles including all tests; 23-25 mpg in normal country and suburban use.

Speedo Error;

Indicated mph	30	40	50	60	70	80
Actual mph	32	42	52	62	73	83

ACCELERATION CHART

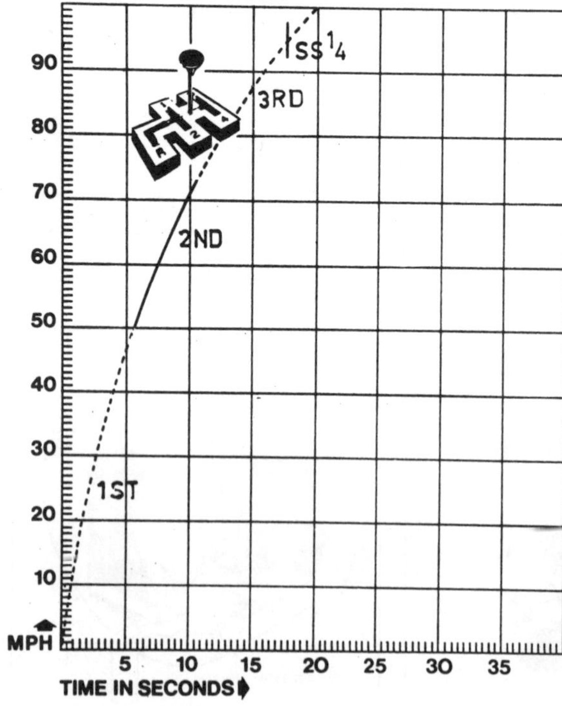

HOW JAGUAR COMPARES

MAXIMUM SPEED (mean) M.P.H.
70 80 90 100 110 120 130
Jaguar E-type ($8389)
Falcon GT ($4725)
Porsche 911T ($9953)

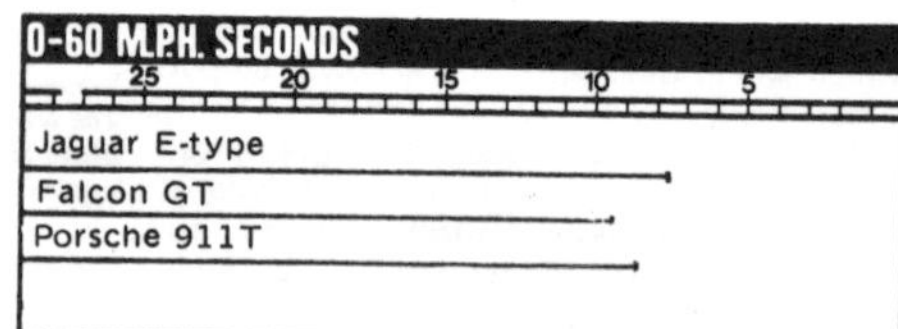

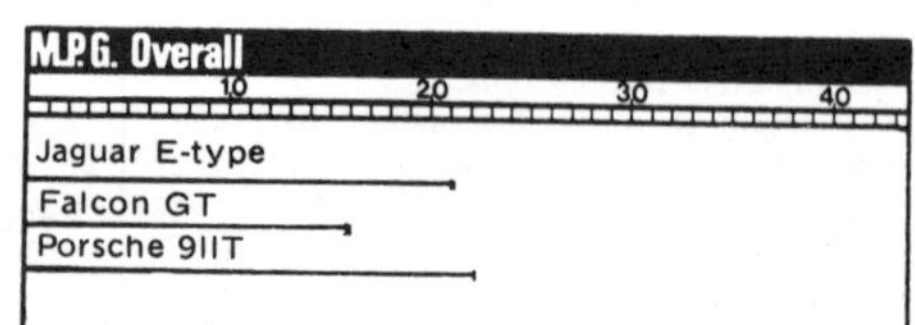

STANDING START ¼ MILE (secs)
20 10
Jaguar E-type
Falcon GT
Porsche 911T

JAGUAR E-TYPE COUPE

Towering performance, superb braking and sexy good looks make the ageing E-type an unforgettable motor car

E—types are old hat. Anyone with even a sketchy interest in motor cars knows that Jaguar's voluptuous speedster has been around nigh on 10 years.

Despite that, the E—Type is still the head—turningest, crowd—stoppingest glamour car around.

It may not have the exotic, way—out specifications of a Lamborghini Miura, or Ferrari GTB4 or Maserati Ghibli. But for sheer "presence" it is unbeatable.

We were fortunate to be able to put close on a thousand miles on a new E—type coupe recently, and it impressed us from the moment we climbed aboard until the moment we regretfully handed it back to British Leyland.

It impressed us with its comfort (we have reservations there, but more about that later), it's effortless performance, great handling and roadholding, and enormously powerful brakes.

We drove it from Melbourne to Sydney on an extremely hot day, and even "loafing" we covered the distance in about nine hours. Of course loafing in an E—type is anything up to 100 mph,and in fact we had the speedo hovering around the 90-100 mark for much of the way.

The most impressive facet of the E is the absolute ease of its performance. The Falcon GT — which performs about equally — makes by comparison a great song—and—dance when it is driven fast. The Jaguar's towering performance is achieved with consummate ease, and considerably more silence than the GT.

Considering its performance, fabulous looks, comfort and

appointments, we think that it is a car in the best Jaguàr traditions. When you also consider that it costs $8389 it begins to look an even better buy — and this after almost 10 years in existence.

The E—type was, when it went on sale almost a decade ago, a car that confronted the Ferrari/Maserati clan head on but at a fraction of the price.

Today, there are many other cars that do this, but all of them are more expensive that the E. Which means of course that it is in many respects, a bargain.

The current E differs from the original car in that it's engine is 4.2 litres, against 3.8.

The engine is of course, the legendary XK double ohc that powered C and D—types to victory at Le Mans. In the E it produces 265 bhp at 5400 and 283 lb. ft. of torque at 4000 rpm.

The engine is a long—stroke design — it was conceived and put into production long before the current fad for short stroke grew popular — so that it has enormous flexibility and enough low—speed torque despite "tall" gearing, to make around—city trickling and freeway loafing an absolute breeze.

The test car was fitted with the standard four—speed manual transmission that proved to be excellent in use. The weak link in Jaguar's drive train has traditionally been the manual transmission, but this latest 'box is beyond reproach. The radios are "right", the movement smooth and precise, and the synchromesh very strong. It is not a weak link any more.

For those driver's who prefer shiftless motoring, the E—type is available with Borg Warner dual range "8" automatic transmission. This is similar to the unit we experienced in the XJ6 and it is good.

Suspension is all independent — a refined system of wishbones and transverse torsion bars at the front with hydraulic dampers and anti—roll bar.

The rear suspension is more complex — lower wishbones, a half—axle as the upper arm, with trailing lower radius arms, four coil springs and four telescopic dampers to provide the suspension medium.

The system works well. The E—type rides smoothly for a sporty car, and handles all but the choppiest of surfaces with aplomb. Radial ply tyres are standard — the test car was fitted with Dunlop Aquajets — and there is a moderate amount of "thump" over irregularities.

Steering is rack and pinion with 2.5 turns of lock and a 41ft. turning circle. It is wholly in keeping with the car's character — quick, precise, and responsive, but with sufficient well damped "feedback" to keep the driver well informed of changes in the road surface.

The steering wheel itself is big in diameter and thin—rimmed. Alloy spokes and a wooden rim date it somewhat. A smaller, thicker, leather—covered wheel would be more in keeping with the car in this day and age.

Fabulous performance is matched by equally fabulous brakes. Four wheels discs are fitted, and these are carried on the wheel hubs at the front, and inboard, adjacent to the differential at the rear.

The fronts are just under 11in. diameter, the rears are 10in. The circuitry is duplicated, as it necessary by law these days, and a moderate servo—assistance makes heavy application easy.

The sleek body, developed after extensive wind—tunnel tests more than 10 years ago, but strangely still as chic a shape as ever, is made of stressed steel, of a patented monocoque construction with a front sub—frame in tubular high—tensile steel (carrying the engine, front suspension, and forward hinged bonnet and front wings.)

We felt at home with the car the moment we slipped aboard. The cab is a very snug fit, but despite this has sufficient leg and head room to accommodate drivers well over six ft. in height. The seats are adjustable for length and height, and the steering wheel is also adjustable, thereby ensuring a sufficiently wide range of ergonomic variation to ensure comfort for most people.

There is unfortunately, no "dead pedal" for the left foot, so that it is forced to rest, somewhat uncomfortably, on the floor, next to the big transmission tunnel. Other minuses in terms of comfort are the too—thin steering wheel rim (you get used to that) and the fresh air ventilation which is practically non—existent, and as a consequence totally inadequate for Australian summer conditions. Try as we might, with all manner of combinations for the semi—flow—through ventilation, and the wind—down windows, we weren't able to get a satisfactory arrangement.

The ambient temperature for most of the time we had the car was about 80, but our Melbourne—Sydney run was done in 100 deg. heat, which made the Jaguar's cab pretty unbearable.

(Continued on page 50)

TOP: E-type's very best angle is full profile in which voluptuous shape is most evident.

RIGHT: Beautiful twin-cam, long-stroke motor is visual delight, and quite straightforward. It produces 265 bhp at 5400 rpm, 283 lb. ft. of torque at 4000 rpm.

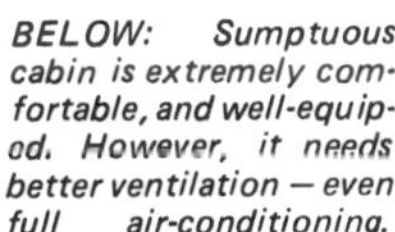

BELOW: Sumptuous cabin is extremely comfortable, and well-equipped. However, it needs better ventilation — even full air-conditioning.

E-TYPE JAG.

(Continued from page 48)

The fact that the car doesn't have those much—maligned swivelling quarter vents added to our discomfort, and we finally resolved that any Australian who bought an E—type coupe or 2—plus—2 without specifying air-conditioning was making a grave mistake.

Occupants are located in such close proximity to the big engine and transmission that the cabin would be hot even in wintery conditions, with the result that air conditioning would be a year round "must".

Dunlopillo padding — is excellent. The seats look nothing special, but they serve their occupants very well over both short and long distances.

Naturally, the car doesn't roll much anyway, and the big sills and close—fitting doors keep people in place. But stiff backs and tender backsides just aren't a part of the E—type picture.

Instrumentation is very comprehensive and traditionally arranged on the black vinyl—covered dash.

Directly in front of the driver and visible through the top half of the wood—rim wheel are matching tachometer and speedo, the former reading to 6000 rpm, and the latter to 160 mph.

Ranged across the dash centre are gauges for fuel, water, amps and oil pressure, together with a small, but painfully—accurate clock.

Beneath that clutch of instruments is arranged a line of tumbler switches for hazard warning four-way flashers, map, interior side, and headlights, two—speed wipers, washer, and fan.

The controls for fresh—air inlet are located on either side of the dash centre, and they're unlike anything we've ever seen before. What's more they don't work particularly well, as we've already explained.

Before the passenger is located the world's smallest glove—compartment (lockable) with just enough room for — you guessed it — a pair of gloves.

Fortunately, there's additional stowage space in a cubby between the seats, beneath a padded centre flap.

Behind the seats is a large luggage area, which can be further enlarged by lowering the forwardmost panel, which when upright, forms a bulkhead to stop luggage catapulting under heavy braking.

The luggage area is protected by rubber and chrome rubbing strips, which tended to turn up and catch in our luggage.

The load area is sufficiently large to take the luggage of two people. week.

Access to the luggage area is gained through a side—hinged back door, the release catch for which is located by the driver's seat. The door swings left and is locked in place by an articulated bow.

From a practicality viewpoint, the E—type stands up very well. It is further enhanced by the forward—hinged bonnet which tilts to reveal not only the engine but the entire front suspension, thus making routine service extremely easy.

It's an easy car to drive. The position behind the wheel is "right", although forward visibility is hampered by the attenuated bonnet line and the enormous power bulge right down the centre of the bonnet.

A couple of times we misjudged the length of the car's bonnet and fetched it up (gently) against obstacles.

We learnt our lesson early and allowed ourselves a very wide safety margin thereafter.

The car starts easily without choke and drives very sweetly, slipping through the gears without effort (although the clutch is on the heavy side) and generally responding like a true thoroughbred.

The car is absolutely no effort to drive and visibility to the rear is (surprisingly) not as restricted as the rakish fastback and smallish rear window suggests.

On the open road the coupe is in its true element, eating the miles with an insatiable 100 mph appetite. We could cruise at 100 mph continuously and the oil and temperature gauges would never budge from their proper marks, despite the high ambient temperatures.

In short bursts we ran it higher, reaching 125 on one appropriately straight stretch. Even at 125, the E—type still had tons in reserve, and should run close to 140 mph.

The car is an almost neutral steerer, seemingly unaffected by closure of the throttle in corners, and quite content to whistle around corners at any speed the driver chooses. It gives a feeling of enormous security, and we never once succeeded in wrong—footing the car.

The suspension works well, soaking up bumps smoothly and generally, with great silence. Unfortunately, the test car developed an undiagnosed rattle that spoiled the limber, cat—like effect otherwise created.

The brakes worked fabulously well. Closing speeds in a car capable of ton—up cruising have to be judged very carefully, and once or twice we found ourselves narrowing the gap much too rapidly. It was then that we appreciated the enormous power of those four—wheel discs which washed off speed with ridiculous ease.

Cruising in this manner the car returned about 20 mpg — which gives, on its 14—gallon tank a modest range of 280 miles. Driven more sedately, the car will return 23 or more mpg, which is a tacit compliment to the slippery tunnel—tested shape.

The E—type is a perfect "poser's" car. It turned more heads than any car we've driven, despite the familiarity of its shape. But it is no cream—puff. Point it up a fast winding road and it will lay down a time for which no apology is needed. It is a sleek, fat cat, with muscles where they are needed. We enjoyed driving it, despite the 10 year wait. Let's hope we don't have to wait so long for the much—rumoured, long—awaited V12 F—type, XL12, or whatever it might be called. ■

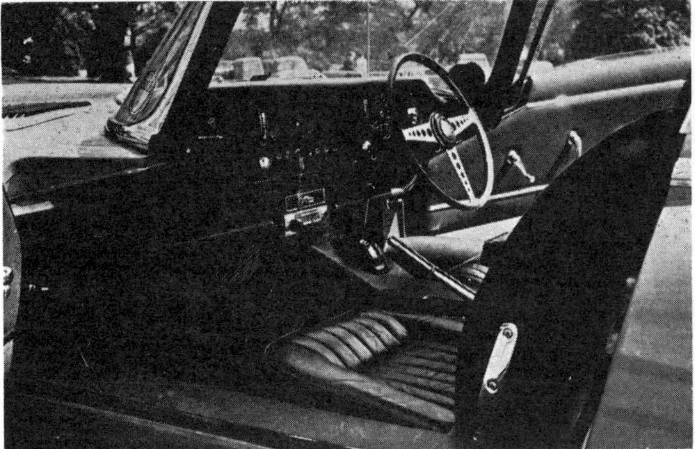

Continued from page 34

Comfort and controls

Not only does the E-type offer a lot of performance for the money, but it is lavishly equipped as well. We have dealt adequately with the seating capacity, which is sufficient to carry a six-footer crosswise in the back seat for several hours, but should mention that the seats are well upholstered and nicely shaped to remain comfortable. The 2 + 2 has folding backrests, of course, so the optional reclining backrest mechanism of the two-seater is not available. If there are two people in the car the back of the rear seat can be folded flat to make a very large luggage area, reached either through the main doors or through the nearside-hinged rear door. The spare wheel and fuel tank are under the floor at the back, and the inboard discs are reached via an inspection hatch in the floor.

Two catches inside the car release the front hinged bonnet, which swings up to give good access to the engine and front suspension. Because the nose is long the bonnet cannot open very high, and one has to reach in a long way to check the water level.

Perhaps we are getting used to low-slung cars—even the saloons are getting on that way now—but ease of entry did not bring to mind any adverse comment like it did four years ago, when the E-type was completely new. From the driving seat one has an excellent forward view, slightly marred by the fact that there is a good foot of bonnet beyond the furthest visible point. The rear window is deeper than on the two-seat coupé, but still accurate reversing needs a little practice.

Ventilation is still not the car's strongest point although a new system has been fitted. Twin controls on the fascia supply a moderate amount of hot or cold air to the legs, aided by a quiet two-speed booster. Still this was hardly enough to ventilate the car thoroughly, although it does help to open the rear quarterlight-type windows. The E-type is exceptionally quiet up to 110 mph when the windows are shut, but opening a main window introduces buffeting inside the cockpit as well as a sharp rise in noise level.

The instruments are clear and well laid out, starting with the speedometer and rev-counter directly in front of the driver and seen through the three-spoke alloy and wood wheel. A small electric clock and a trip meter are included. Across the central console are located the water temperature and oil pressure gauges, master lighting switch, fuel gauge and ammeter. There is

a warning light for low petrol level, and the choke is controlled by a three-position sliding lever matched by a heating combination control on the left. There are also warning lights for indicators, handbrake application or hydraulic fluid level (a dual hydraulic system is fitted for safety), and choke application.

The toggle switches, which move upwards, are placed in a row and although identified by illuminated lettering, need to be memorised. They operate the electric screen washers, two-speed wipers, map light, heater fan, two-level fascia lighting, and the interior light. A cigarette lighter is fitted.

There can hardly be any doubt that the 2 + 2 E-type is comprehensively equipped and comfortable. And fast, and safe, and good looking . . . it is a fabulous car for the family man. Superb for long fast journeys, and not even unwieldy in town once you get used to the long bonnet and poor (40 foot) turning circle. With manual transmission this version is claimed to do 145 mph and reach 100 mph in 18.2 seconds, which should please the kids no end.

M.L.C.

SPECIFICATION

ENGINE

Six cylinders in line; bore 92.07 mm, stroke 106 mm. Cubic capacity 4235 cc. Compression ratio 9:1. Maximum power 265 bhp (gross) at 5400 rpm; maximum torque 283 lb ft at 4000 rpm. Twin overhead camshafts. Three SU HD8 carburettors, electric SU petrol pump. Tank capacity 14 gallons (63.6 litres). Water cooling system 32 pints with pump, electric fan and thermostat. Sump capacity 15 pints. 12V 57 amp hr battery. Grease points, 17 every 6000 miles.

TRANSMISSION

Borg Warner 8 three-speed automatic with torque converter, with 2.88 final drive ratio. Standard equipment four-speed all synchromesh, with 3.07 final drive ratio. Powr-Lok limited slip differential standard fitting.

CHASSIS

Integral monocoque construction. Suspension, front: independent by wishbones and torsion bar, anti-roll bar, telescopic dampers. Rear: independent by trailing arms with lower transverse link, fixed-length driveshafts, twin coil spring/damper units. Anti-roll bar. Twin circuit hydraulic brakes with servo-assistance; 11-in discs at front, 10-in dia discs at rear. Rack and pinion steering. Steering wheel 16-in dia, 2.6 turns lock to lock. Centre-lock 72 spoke wire wheels, Dunlop SP41 HR tyres size 185-15.

DIMENSIONS

	ft	ins
Wheelbase	8	9
Track, front	4	2.25
Track, rear	4	2.25
Overall length	15	4.75
Overall width	5	4
Overall height	4	2.5
Ground clearance		5.5
Turning circle	39	6
Kerb weight	27.5 cwt	

PERFORMANCE

Mph	secs
0 - 30	4.3
0 - 40	5.9
0 - 50	6.9
0 - 60	9.1
0 - 70	11.1
0 - 80	14.0
0 - 90	17.9
0 - 100	21.5
Speeds in gears	
Low	55 mph
Intermediate	87 mph
High	138 mph
Fuel consumption	18.5 mpg
Price, with tax	£2284
Price as tested	£2427

Honestly - it really is the V12!

Jaguar's new V12 puts the E-type back in the 150mph class ▸

Honestly - it really is the V12!

SOME OF MY MORE highly sexually charged friends aver that anticipation is better than realisation, the exhilaration of the chase often proving more satisfying than the eventual conquest. When the gentleman from the Jaguar press office telephoned to say would I come up to Coventry to have a look at their new V12 E-type I wondered if the realisation of my five-year-long anticipation would be satisfying. As a Jaguarophile of long standing I am happy to say that the answer is yes, even if it is a slightly qualified yes.

Perhaps it would be best to begin at the beginning. Rumours of a V12 Jaguar started in the early '60s, quite correctly as it transpired because a V12 engine was being developed. As Jaguar now admit, this engine was intended for a return to the racing scene and featured four overhead cams, hemi-heads, fuel injection and all the gubbins necessary for producing 500bhp at 8000rpm from 5litres, a figure which it achieved on the test bed. However, the racing programme was abandoned and the decision taken to produce a V12 for road use as an eventual replacement for the XK engine which has stood Jaguar in good stead since 1948. Over 370,000 XK engines have been produced to date and it stays in production alongside the V12 unit.

The qualification I spoke about earlier comes when the design of the V12 is studied, for it is pretty obvious that this engine will not make its mark on the racing scene as the XK did—it's a production engine pure and simple. As Harry Mundy emphatically states 'Forget all about racing—there is no way this can be made into a racing unit.' Mundy is Chief Designer–Power Units at Jaguar and was responsible for the design along with Bill Heynes, Claude Baily and Wally Hassan. Their design brief was to produce a V12 which was quieter, smoother, had more torque and more power than any XK engine had ever produced. The highest genuine figure seen for an XK engine was 325bhp in competition tune, and this was the starting point for the V12. A V12 was decided upon partly for prestige (it will be the only volume production V12 in the world) and partly for the excellent balance of a 12; there is no primary or secondary imbalance and the three-plane crankshaft has good torsional characteristics. Jaguar also point out that it is possible to produce a smaller engine from this basic design, but they hasten to point out that there is no application in mind for a smaller unit at present. Since taxation in some countries is weighted heavily against cars over 2.8litres it seems possible that a variant of this size might be developed.

A variety of different configurations were tried during development, including the twin-cam-per-bank, hemi-head layout of the racing unit, as well as a variety of other head designs. Each one was tried on single-cylinder test engines but after exhaustive testing it was decided that a single cam per bank with a flat cylinder head and the combustion chamber in the piston crown was the best configuration to suit the design brief. This obviously does not have the power potential of some other designs but it meets all the requirements for a high-performance road engine. More important, it was able to meet the current US air pollution regulations which became more stringent during the development of the V12, thus helping to delay its announcement by probably over a year. Since more than 75percent of Jaguar production goes to the States they must of course meet every demand made upon them in the US.

Items that did not change from the original concept of a V12 were the 60deg. angle of the cylinder banks and the bore and stroke of 90 by 70mm. This is very oversquare, giving the engine much higher revving capabilities than the XK unit; in its first application on the Series Three E-type the engine is red lined at 6500rpm but there is more to come if necessary. Valve crash is not reached until a theoretical 7840rpm.

Both cast-iron and aluminium blocks were cast during development as it was originally anticipated that an aluminium block would be too noisy but to everyone's surprise the alloy block engine was no noisier on test, so it was quickly decided to go to a sand-cast aluminium alloy LM25 for both heads and block; many other items like the sump, timing case and inlet manifolds are also aluminium, while the tappet blocks are pressure die-cast aluminium. The only cast-iron items are the camshafts and bearing caps. Even with all the aluminium components the engine weighs a hefty 680lb—about 80lb more than the 4.2litre XK engine. The switch from twin cams per bank to single resulted in a weight saving of 22lb per head; it also gave much more under-bonnet room to locate the ancillaries.

The heron head configuration was found to have exceptionally good effect on exhaust emission levels, and even with an initial compression ratio of 10.6 to 1 the engine ran well on 99octane fuel. Subsequent reductions to 10 to 1 and finally 9 to 1 were needed to assist further with the emission problem and the engine will now run on 97octane fuel—useful on an engine which is claimed to average between 13 and 18mpg! Surprisingly, other manufacturers are in all sorts of trouble with bowl-in-piston engines, particularly with noise and pollution. There is talk that Ford and Rover will have to abandon their b-i-p engines if pollution laws become stricter. The valves are placed vertically in line, operated directly by the camshafts which have no bearings, simply running in the aluminium material of the detachable tappet block. Originally the dished pistons had a deep combustion chamber, but since the piston reached high in the head, recesses had to be cut in the edges of the pistons to clear the valves. A later design, which was finalised, gave a shallower, wider combustion chamber and obviated the need for valve cut-outs; it also improved the power output. A great deal of research was made into spark plug position and it was discovered that the best position was for the plug to be as near the centre of the combustion chamber as possible.

The I-section connecting rods are in EN 16T steel, as is the crankshaft, which is Tuftrided for hardness and strength. It has seven main bearings, each three inches in diameter. The camshafts are driven by a duplex chain on the front of the engine for no other reason than Jaguar have found them to be reliable and reasonably silent. A complicated system of location, damping and tensioning is used but Jaguar feel this layout is preferable to the extra engine length that would result if the now fashionable exposed belts were used. Both sides of a chain can be used, unlike belts, so the outer surface of the V12 chain is used to drive the jackshaft.

One of Sir William Lyons' stipulations about the V12 was that the sweeping lines of the E-type bonnet should not be spoiled by protuberances from any new engine, so the usual vee engine practice of fitting the carburettors in the centre of the vee had to be abandoned. Placing of the four Zenith 175CDSE carburettors outside the vee has given a bonus in torque, for the long induction pipes give a good ram effect from low revs. Fuel injection

can be accommodated on this engine but all the current injection systems have a severe pollution problem and cannot be entertained on the V12 at present, although work is continuing.

Lubrication is by a crescent-type oil pump similar to the type used in automatic transmissions; since the inner gear is keyed to the crankshaft the complication of an oil pump drive is eliminated. Oil cooling is looked after by a cooler beneath the front of the sump which is in fact cooled by the water which is returning from the base of the radiator to the water pump. Rather surprisingly, perhaps, the oil temperature is reduced by 22deg C by this method yet water temperature rises only one deg C. The ignition is something of a breakthrough. Jaguar has become the first manufacturer to fit the Lucas Opus electronic ignition system which has been developed from the type used on Formula One cars. It provides up to 700 sparks a second (against the 400 of a make-and-break distributor) and there are no moving parts to wear so ignition will be unchanged over high mileages—a major factor in keeping the engine 'clean' from a pollution standpoint over long distances.

There are many other aspects of the Jaguar engine I would love to discuss but sheer space prevents further amplification at this stage. Since Jaguar's own description of the engine covers some 27 closely typed pages the task is almost impossible. It is undoubtedly a masterpiece of production engineering to even contemplate building this unit. I was able to visit the old Daimler works in Coventry, which alas no longer builds cars, being devoted largely to assembly of the XK and V12 engines. One section of the factory has been completely re-tooled at a cost of £3,000,000 to build the V12 and at the time of my visit about 50 engines a week were being produced while the operatives became accustomed to the new unit. This will step up to around 170 units a week soon and ultimately over 500 a week will pour out of the factory. Although a great deal of automation has been introduced, with automatic transfer machines doing many of the machining and drilling operations, there is still a great deal of hand work done, such as port grinding, valve fitting and so on. It is a pleasure to see the intricate castings being lovingly worked on and carefully assembled. All engines are bench-tested for proper performance over a period of about an hour at up to 2500rpm and are then checked for power at 3000rpm.

The cars

Initially the V12 will only be available in the E-type range, but Jaguar make no secret of the fact that it will ultimately appear in the XJ6, but with the waiting list already 12 months long there will be no great rush to bring out a V12 XJ6. Mid-1972 was the earliest guess anyone from Jaguar would make.

Although the Series Three E-type looks much the same as its predecessors at a glance, there have been numerous modifications made to the range. For a start the short eight-foot wheelbase models have all been dropped, only the longer 8ft 9in chassis of the two-plus-two now being available. Additionally, the coupé two-seater has been dropped completely—more's the pity, as this to my mind was the most aesthetically pleasing and practical of the E-type variants. So now there are two basic models: the roadster and the two-plus-two on the long-wheelbase chassis, which are available with either the 4.2litre XK six-cylinder engine or the V12 and a choice of manual or automatic transmission. The extra wheelbase on the roadster has been utilised to increase the passenger space, the doors being lengthened appropriately. A lidded luggage box is fitted behind the seats to complement the rear boot which remains unchanged. The seats can be reclined more on the new roadster now that the upper edge of the rear body section has been moved back nine inches. The two-plus-two interior remains virtually unchanged.

Mechanically there have been several changes. The front suspension is now very similar to that of the XJ6 with a small amount of anti-dive built in. Ventilated discs are fitted on the front wheels but the inboard rear discs remain solid. Power-assisted steering is now standard equipment on all V12 models and the turning circle has been reduced to 36ft. New six-inch-wide pressed-steel wheels with Dunlop SP Sport tyres are now standard on all models with wire wheels as an option; the new wheels help to increase the track by 4.25in at the front and 3.5in at the rear. The Model 12 Borg-Warner automatic transmission is available on all models now, replacing the Model 8 which was previously available only on the two-plus-two. The same four-speed manual gearbox as used on the XK engine is fitted to the V12 but the diameter of the clutch is increased by an inch to 10.5in. The fuel tank is increased in capacity from 14 gallons to 18. The heating and demisting system has been improved by fitting through-flow ventilation on all models.

On the road

An afternoon—even a warm sunny one—in rural Warwickshire is hardly long enough to evaluate such a new car. New because to all intents and purposes the Series Three E-type *is* a new car. Only a quartet of two-plus-twos were available for test, none of the potentially more exciting roadsters being ready yet. However, I was able to try both the manual and automatic versions.

First impressions on starting the V12 were of the silence and smoothness of the V12. It starts first time and immediately settles down to a quiet, even tick-over with none of the Ferrari and Lamborghini-like noises I have come to expect from V12s; no thrashing of timing chains, no ticker-ticker from tappets or clattering from dozens of valves opening and closing, just a gentle murmur. Moving the automatic lever to D and motoring out onto the open

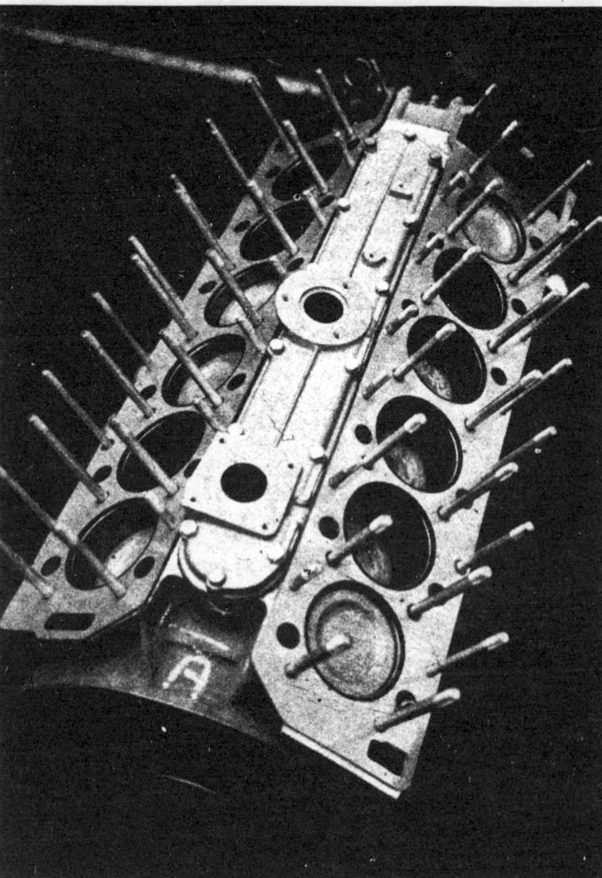

The sectioned view of one bank of Jaguar's V12 (far left) shows the beefy seven-bearing crank, steel I-section rods, the big 90mm-bore pistons with the combustion chambers in the top, the in-line vertical valves and the chain-driven camshaft. Also shown are the long induction pipes from the twin Zenith carburettors. The roadster (left) with its hardtop in place looks beautifully proportioned and conceals its extra nine inches of wheel-base very effectively. Just to prove that Jaguar are actually building the Series Three E-type, this shot (top) shows a 2 + 2 on the line. The V12 block (bottom) shows the piston, combustion chambers and camshaft drives

road did not dispel the first impression: all was silence. When the engine was warm and a clear stretch of road appeared I floored the throttle and waited for the kick in the back; the Borg-Warner gremlins slowly selected second and the car began to surge forward —quickly but not as rapidly as I would have expected. However, a glance at the speedo showed 100mph on the clock already and I prudently eased off, guiltily glancing in the mirror. As the afternoon wore on I began to realise how deceptive this engine is; with only 272bhp (DIN) at 5850rpm it ought not to have been much quicker than the earlier 2 + 2 models but it obviously was. Without having any opportunity to take figures I would say the V12 two-plus-two is about as fast as the production 3.8 coupé of 1962, which may not seem much in the way of progress but the two-plus-two is a good deal heavier and the pollution equipment does nothing for the power output.

When I switched to a manual gearbox two-plus-two I was much happier because I felt more inclined to use the power and throw the car around. A quick check on speeds in the gears showed 52, 80 and 110 just before the red line, and a deliciously illegal burst up to 130 in top indicated that Jaguar's claim of a 150mph top speed could probably be substantiated. The tachometer showed just under 5000rpm at this speed. On the 3.3 to one axle which is standard in the UK, 1000rpm in top equals 22.9mph, so 150mph should be possible at just over 6500rpm. I satisfied myself that the engine would spin comfortably to this figure with far less commotion than the XK engine makes at lower revs. It remained smooth, quiet and utterly docile. The most impressive aspect of the engine is its massive torque. From 10mph in top gear the car will pull away without a shudder or any sign of protest—it just eases away impressively, gathering speed the whole time. It should be possible to start away from rest in top gear, but I did not subject the car to that indignity.

The handling of the two-plus-two has undoubtedly improved over its predecessor because the Series Three can be tossed around remarkably quickly, the power steering giving just the right amount of assistance, yet retaining sufficient feel. The anti-dive works well, for the car remains remarkably level under panic braking; not unnaturally the brakes began to wilt towards the end of a hectic afternoon, smelling evilly and making protestations by groaning and, on one occasion, locking the front wheels. However, if any private owner drove like that all the time he would soon end in gaol or the cemetery anyway.

As I said right at the beginning there is a tinge of regret that the V12 is not a fire-breathing, hemi-headed, bellowing monster that is going to sweep the Porsches and Ferraris off the race tracks, or blast down the autostradi of Italy, proudly elbowing Lambos into the slow lane. Commonsense dictates that the emphasis on torque and quietness is the only way to go in these restrictive days. All the same I'm looking forward to giving a V12 roadster its head in the not-too-distant future.

Deliveries in the UK are going to take second place to those dollar-earning exports but in the meantime you can place your order sure in the knowledge that Jaguar have done it again. ●

The price of clean air

Continued from page 45

In equipping their US export cars with this feature, Jaguar are anticipating a 1971 Californian regulation. The object is to prevent petrol vapour escaping from either the fuel tank or the carburettor float-chambers in to the atmosphere. This is achieved in the the carburettors by venting the float chambers to the engine side of the air-cleaner element which virtually seals off any vapour from the atmosphere while the engine is at rest. Manifold suction inspires any fumes during running.

Much more elaborate arrangements are necessary for the fuel tank. The filler cap itself is sealed and the only way in which vapour can escape is via three vent pipes at the extreme corners of the tank. These three pipes go to a fuel-expansion tank that has a top vent connected to a special canister in the engine compartment. This canister contains activated charcoal which absorbs any fuel vapour when the engine is not running.

When the engine is operating a connection to the crank-case breather draws fresh air through the carbon from a vent in the base of the canister. This serves to purge the carbon (which has a negligible effect on mixture strength) by evaporating the fuel trapped in it and drawing it into the induction system.

Inevitably, these emission control measures bring about some reductions in output on the US export cars. These are especially noticeable on the E-type engine, which now has only two carburettors. The following are the gross output figures for the 4.2-litre engines (with the figures for European unmodified engines in brackets):

E-type: 245 (265) b.h.p. at 5,500 (5,400) r.p.m.; 263 (283) lb./ft. torque at 3,000 (4,000) r.p.m.
XJ: 240 (245) b.h.p. at 5,500 (5,400) r.p.m.; 263 (283) lb./ft. torque at 3,000 (3,750) r.p.m.

In addition to these modifications the 1970 E-type and XJ Jaguars include a number of other detailed improvements. Notable among these is a load-shedding device so arranged that all ancillaries are cut off from the main circuit when the starter is engaged to ease the load on the battery. Another new device is a warning buzzer that sounds when the driver's door is closed and the key is left in the ignition, thus avoiding any risk of the car being left with any ancillaries switched on. Other electrical refinements are a provision for illuminating the heater and choke controls and an arrangement by which the US-type, combined side marker and reflectors are now positively illuminated with the side lights.

JAGUAR'S EXOTIC E

(Continued from page 19)

stoppers are fitted all round and they do a remarkable job. The servo assistance helps lighten pedal pressures and during a couple of crash stops from 130 mph the car just seemed to dig into the road and bracing was needed to stop the passenger and driver being thrown through the windscreen. At the front the brakes are mounted on the wheel hubs while the rear discs are fitted inboard adjacent to the differential. Only medium pedal pressures were needed to bring the car to a screaming halt, and at no stage did they lockup.

After the test when I was wending my way home through fairly thick Sydney suburban traffic I could not help but think that in many ways an E-type is unsuitable for this country. There are only a few places were it can be extended and even then there is a high risk element. Unlike the Continent where the magnificently paved autobahns and autostradas roll for hundreds of miles on end and cruising speeds in the vicinity of 120 mph can be reached, the owner of a fast car in this country is lucky if he can average 70 mph from point A to point B.

The performance, finish and handling of the E puts it in a class of its own, on a value for money basis, and it is easy to see why Jaguar have a reputation which is envied by many similar makers today.

Sir William Lyons has applied mass production techniques to the building of quality cars and has been one of the select few ever to use this method successfully. What other car, costing less than £3500, in this country, can exceed 150 mph? #

Viewpoint: Jaguar V-12

BY PATRICK BEDARD

Jaguar draws ever closer to its goal of "a Ferrari for half the price."

Jaguar XK-E serial number 70009 was not the first V-12 ever produced. It was the ninth. And when British-Leyland finally let us take a look, it was sandwiched between an Austin America and a bright orange MG-B in the importer's service garage in New Jersey. There was no trumpet fanfare or drum roll to herald the introduction. Just a couple of mechanics on the far side of the garage pounding on the bottom side of a Rover 3500S and the rushing air sound of an overhead space heater.

But then the Jaguar people don't get much practice at events like this—introducing new cars. They're good for about two new models per decade and, until now, they hadn't unveiled a fresh engine since 1948. So the procedures are a little rusty and without an easily remembered precedent. And besides, this wasn't an official introduction—more like a sneak preview—a chance for *Car and Driver* to do a driving impression of 70009.

"It's not a prototype," we were told, "but then it's not really a production model either." More like a final test car, just to make sure everything is under control before the assembly line is switched on. And we had to promise not to do a full road test on it. "There's nothing wrong with it. Just don't test it."

The guys at British-Leyland who deal with the press are no dummies. They know that the editors of car books are cutthroats, every bit as underhanded as those who sell cars, so, somewhere in the British-Leyland hierarchy, it was decided that all of the meritorious magazines (three, in their estimation) would be handed identical V-12 automatic, 2+2 coupes on the same day. The other two were in California. That way nobody would be "first" and Jaguar wouldn't have to suffer reprisals later from editors who felt they had been slighted.

The V-12 engine has been a fairly well kept secret, about like the Lost Dutchman gold mine. For three or four years (U.S. Jaguar representatives thought it had been under development for 5-7 years) we've known it existed but not where. And not what car it would be introduced in if it were ever introduced at all. So when British-Leyland finally dropped the "What V-12?" attitude, they were immediately asked, "In which car?"

"The XK-E."

"Can you see the difference on the outside?"

"If you know Jaguars."

Once inside the service garage, the discerning eye of the *C/D* staff (there were three of us) soon knew which was 70009. The one with the 6500 rpm redline on the tach, that's which one. Any Jaguar driver who spends all the days of his life looking at a five-grand limit would know the new one immediately.

There are other clues if you look carefully. The grille opening is larger now with an extra scoop below the nose for better cooling and there is a mesh insert in the opening instead of the old crossbar. The fenders are flared too, to make room for the half-inch wider (6-inch) wheels and new low-profile ER70-15 tires—the same combination that is used on the XJ sedan.

Then if you really know your Jaguars you'll notice that the track is wider—4.4 inches in front and 2.8 in back. Heavy stuff. On the other hand, if one Jaguar looks like any other to you, you can walk around to the rear and check for the V-12 emblem on the trunk lid. That's the sure way. But not with 70009. It was a secret car. Had to be. There were two full months until the New York Auto Show introduction. So the Jaguar people had taken the V-12 sign off. They'd been driving the car all around, taking it home nights, and without the sign it was just another E-type. The *hoi polloi* didn't know the difference.

But that solved only half the problem. What to do with the emblem itself? It couldn't be left lying around because the wrong person might see it and know that there was a V-12 something somewhere. Or somebody around the shop might "pinch" it and screw it onto his Triumph. The obvious answer was to hide it. So the chief Public Relations man, who had it removed in the first place, entrusted it to one of his minions for secreting away somewhere only he would know. And then the PR man forgot who he gave it to. It was supposed to reappear when we arrived. It clearly *had* to be on for photography—the other magazines were getting V-12s on their cars—but it was too well hidden and a new one had to be ordered.

While the discerning editorial eye was peering beneath 70009's hood, Mike Dale, British-Leyland Motors, Inc. Vice-President of Sales, was across the driveway, squirming around in the driver's seat of a mustard yellow Triumph Stag. You can make a case for Dale either way. He really is a car nut—a top-down, wire-wheel, Koni-shock kind of car nut—and he talks a lot about racing his bug-eye Sprite, not because he thinks it will impress anybody, but because that's where his mind lives. You might say he's the perfect man to be Vice-President of Sales for the likes of Spitfires, TR-6s, MGs and Jaguars because they are his kind of cars. On the other hand, since he likes them so much he's not likely to be a voice crying in the wilderness to get them modernized out of the Fifties. But never mind that. He is rare among auto executives because he's enthusiastic, he knows answers and he doesn't hedge when you ask him a question.

Of course he's happy about the V-12. "That's the kind of car we're selling." He has said in the past that, "A Jaguar is a Ferrari for half the price" and if that were true in substance before, it's even more valid now that the V-12 has arrived. He allowed that Jaguar's real competition is Porsche. "Forty percent of the E-type buyers also considered a Porsche before they signed the order form. Only 20 percent look at Mercedes. Those who buy an XK-E instead of a Corvette do so because they want something out of the ordinary."

His idea is that the Jaguar customer wants something exotic and the V-12 will do the job. The price will go up. "About $7000 for the roadster. Power steering will be standard equipment—it's extra now." The current 6-cylinder E-type roadster sells for $5734 plus $160 for power steering. That means the V-12 carries about an $1100 tariff. But if Dale is right, if Porsche is the chief competitor, then the price hike won't hurt because you can't buy much of a Porsche for $7000.

The E-type is built almost exclusively for the American market. Production was the highest ever this past year, 750 cars per month, 90% of which were sent to the U.S., and Dale figures the V-12 will create enough demand to sell even more this year if the factory can make them.

But he's not ruling out the Six. Right now there are still a number of 6-cylinder E-types in stock and there are no definite plans to build more. But the engine will continue in production for the XJ, and if a demand should arise for 6-cylinder E-types, the factory will just switch over and build a batch of them. "Jaguar is still a low volume builder and they can do that."

59

The low volume is what makes the V-12 feasible too. Jaguar is not in the business of building everyman's car; it assembles a limited number of cars for those who want something a little bit exclusive and can afford it. As Dale explained this he looked down at 70009, its hood up, and the V-12 almost hidden under a tangle of intake manifolds, air injection tubing, ignition wires and complex carburetor linkage. "It's not much for service, " he observed, "but then the Six wasn't either." The feeling around British-Leyland is that the thought of a V-12 will be a far greater plus than the service hassle will be a minus in the customers' minds. Traditionalism is not yet dead.

The real issue, then, is whether or not the V-12 does memorable things. Can it heat up the wealthy sports car buyer's heart cockles more than a Porsche would? It has to do more than just move the car about—the Six did that—and it should do more than just make a quick car because an American-style V-8 would have produced as much power at a whole lot less cost. The V-12 has to be exciting in a way that a simpler engine wouldn't be, if it is to be a success at an $1100 higher price.

We couldn't wait to hear what it sounded like. V-12s are supposed to make your hair stand on end, you know. Well, the Jaguar doesn't. It's too dignified. But you'll never confuse it with the Six. At idle, a homogenous stream of exhaust pulses flow out of the tailpipe so that it doesn't even sound like an engine. The pulses are soft and one blends into the next to make a purring sound. The tachometer says 700 rpm but it sounds like twice that. If you were expecting it to be like a Ferrari, forget it. Mechanical noise from the engine is nil and the exhaust never shrieks. In fact, when you stand on it, it sounds like two small Jaguars more than anything else. Which perhaps makes sense when you realize that some of the key men in the design of the old XK Six, Walter Hassan for one, are still at Jaguar and supervised the V-12's birth.

It also makes sense that one of the first things we wanted to do with 70009 after breaking it loose from the guys at British-Leyland was to hurl it around a little bit and see what it was up to. It's plenty quick—a whole lot more so than the approximate increase of 40 advertised horsepower would lead you to believe. It's not highly tuned and yet the retarded timing (for emission control) kills off the bottom end, so that it suddenly becomes appreciably stronger as it approaches 3000 rpm and then continues to build right up to 6000, and it doesn't drop off noticeably at the redline. Since we promised not to do a road test, we can't give performance figures at this time and the automatic transmission would make them seem less impressive if we did. We expect, however, that a 4-speed V-12 will turn the quarter-mile in the 14.7-second range at about 97 mph and will have a top speed of 130-140 mph.

The Jaguar is certainly more tractable than the 911S. Using the manual choke, it starts easily in New York's wintertime temperatures and, unlike the XK Six, it produces enough power when it's cold so that you can immediately drive away. And it's free of annoying habits in all ranges of operation. At cruising speeds, 50 mph or above, you definitely hear the engine—a smooth hum rather than a hard mechanical sound—and it gets louder as speed increases, but, for a sports car, it never reaches an unreasonable level. The exhaust sound is audible only as you approach wide open throttle. Naturally it produces power in an uncommonly smooth flow, anybody who drives it will tell you that—at great length. What are V-12s for? But, like most emission-controlled cars you've driven, it still shakes when idling with the automatic transmission in gear.

With the addition of the V-12, the E-type has also undergone a suspension redesign. As mentioned earlier, the track is considerably wider, especially in the front, where the engineers have lengthened the control arms and increased the anti-dive. The front brakes have also been revised with new ventilated rotors. The rear disc brakes have not been changed but they should be more fade resistant because air cooling ducts have been added. A complete evaluation of the handling and brakes will appear in an upcoming issue as soon as a proper car is available.

Really, quite a few more changes than just a new engine have been made to the E-type. The whole model line-up has been revised. There will be only two body styles from now on—the roadster and the 2+2 coupe. The old 2-passenger coupe is gone.

PHOTOGRAPHY: GENE BUTERA

Along with it went the short, 96-inch wheelbase of the roadster and coupe. The new roadsters will share the 105-inch wheelbase chassis with the 2+2. Contrary to what you might think, lengthening the car had nothing to do with the new engine; all of the increase takes place in the cockpit. From the E-type's day of introduction in 1961 there have been leg room complaints and Jaguar has finally taken action on them in a big way. Even the NBA will be satisfied. About leg room, that is.

As far as the basic car is concerned, automotive activists could plead a strong case for euthanasia. It's an *old* car, it's uncomfortable and every year it gets uglier. Remember how beautiful the first E-types were with their small grille openings, faired in headlights and small taillights? It's true that some of those features did not find favor with the National Highway Safety Bureau but why did Jaguar always have to take the easy way out? Like stuffing bigger headlights into the old small openings and hanging the taillights below the rear bumper like something from J.C. Whitney. The taillights *have* been smoothed-in on the V-12 but the rudely opened grille and the flaired fenders are clumsy additions in what has become the Jaguar tradition. The driver still has nowhere to rest his left foot and the seats are carry-overs from the days when a good bucket seat was one that had a backrest shaped like half of a nail keg, never mind what it felt like.

From a mechanical viewpoint, the new E-type is more sophisticated than ever and Jaguar has to be admired for its appreciation of mechanical esthetics—and the E-type will once again find itself in the limelight. The engine's only fault is that it makes the *car* look old.

Possibly Jaguar's last new engine before Uncle Sam outlaws everything but solar batteries.

Jaguar's new engine is an all-aluminum 60° V-12 displacing 326 cubic inches. It is an over-square design—3.54-in. bore, 2.76-in. stroke—has a 9.0-to-one compression ratio and one overhead camshaft per bank of cylinders. Advertised horsepower had not been released by press time but is expected to be about 285, up 39 hp over the 258 cu.in. Six. Without air cleaners and mufflers gross output on the dynamometer is 315 hp at 6200 rpm and 349 lb-ft of torque at 3800 rpm.

Most of the engine's aluminum components, including the block and heads, are sand cast. For stiffness, the block is heavily ribbed and has a skirt which extends well below the crankshaft centerline. Wet cylinder liners of cast iron are used and are held in position by the clamping force of the cylinder head. The 6-throw crankshaft is of forged steel, tuftrided for hardness, and rotating on seven journal-type main bearings. The 3-ring pistons are die-cast aluminum with full-floating pins. A single timing chain at the front of the engine drives both cams and the distributor-drive jackshaft between the cylinder banks. Cogged belts were rejected for this application because two of them would have been required, one for each bank, and they would have added too much length to the engine.

Since Jaguar is no longer serious about racing, and exhaust emission considerations are more important than ultimate horsepower these days, the V-12 has been designed as a street engine with good pulling power in the lower speed ranges so that it will be compatible with an automatic transmission. For these conditions, double overhead cams and hemispherical combustion chambers are expensive and unnecessary complexities. The V-12 has in-line valves operating through bucket-shaped tappets directly off the camshafts. Shims are still used for lash adjustment.

The deck surface of the cylinder head is completely flat so that the combustion chamber is formed by the dished tops of the pistons, much like the 1600cc crossflow Ford used in the Cortina, Capri and Pinto. Jaguar engineers believe that the flat head is more efficient than a wedge for their intended usage and the engine still has a good power potential because the relatively large bores allow room for generous valves. The single cam layout also saves weight. During development, a twin cam version was tested but it added 44 lbs. and considerable bulk to the engine.

A cast iron block was also tried, primarily to determine its effect on engine noise. In testing, it was not quiet enough to be worthwhile and would have added 122 lbs. to the overall weight of the engine. Considering the aluminum production engine's modest 5.3-liter displacement, its overall weight of 680 lbs. (82 lbs. heavier than the XK Six) is not particularly light. And its liquid capacities are astounding—21.5 quarts in the cooling system and 11 quarts of oil in the sump. As a point of interest here, the sump has a built-in oil cooler. Water returning to the block from the bottom of the radiator first passes through a heat exchanger in the front of the oil pan—cooling the oil if it's hot or warming it in cold weather.

Any discussion of induction and exhaust systems must also include emission control techniques. Jaguar has been working for some time with a mechanical fuel injection system but it was unsatisfactory for emissions. Consequently, the V-12 has four Stromberg 175 CD-2 carburetors—the same single-throat side-drafts that are used on the emission controlled Six. Four separate water-heated intake manifolds are used, arranged to feed groups of three adjacent cylinders—and each manifold has its own carburetor. The manifolds feed into round intake ports, have long branch lengths and have been designed for a pronounced ram-tuning effect in the low to medium-speed range.

The exhaust from each bank is collected into two cast iron headers and passed into two exhaust pipes which join into one before the muffler located within the wheelbase. The tailpipes from both sides finally join in a single resonator underneath the trunk floor.

For emission control, in addition to the water-heated intake manifolds, the V-12 uses heated intake air and has an air pump to inject air into the exhaust ports just downstream from the exhaust valve heads. Spark timing is also retarded during low speed operation.

Apart from emissions, 12-cylinder engines traditionally present a unique ignition problem—with a cam-type distributor the dwell angle is so small that it's almost impossible to provide a healthy spark. Ferrari gets around this by having two 6-cylinder distributors, one for each bank. Jaguar's V-12 uses the Lucas OPUS system—similar in operation to that used on Grand Prix cars for the last five or six years. It consists of a single, large diameter, breakerless distributor to trigger a transistor apparatus. The esoteric aspects of the OPUS operation are best left to the service manual but, since it has no contact points or rubbing surfaces, it is expected to last for the life of the car with only occasional cleaning and lubrication. With an eye toward service, the distributor and spark plugs have been located on top of the engine between the banks, obscured only by the complex throttle linkage and air injection plumbing.

While it is impossible to forecast the engine's durability, Jaguar has been doing "environmental testing" in the U.S. for about 10 months and feels confident that there will be no service problems. Knowing Jaguar's habit of keeping its engines in production for upwards of two decades and knowing that the V-12's bore centers are far enough apart to allow for future displacement increases, you might just as well consider this new powerplant a permanent addition to the line. In fact, it could be Jaguar's last new engine before emission control laws force a change to solar batteries.

When we drove the first V12 E-type to hit Australia back in our May issue we licked our lips at the thought of opening the engine right up in a full test. Well, now we've done the full bit—and the engine proved just as tremendous as we expected. But it also showed how far behind the times the rest of the car has fallen

V12
E TYPE
ROAD
TEST

V12 E TYPE... A SWEETER SORT OF PURR!

THE IMMACULATELY clean aerodynamic shape of the original E-type has gradually been eroded.

Things like flared wheel arches to accommodate fatter tyres, increased intake area, pop-eyed headlamps and various bits of chrome have all taken their toll. The evolution has been rather like that of a military aircraft which leaves the drawing board as sleek as its designers can make it and then has hardware tacked on to make it practical for the job it has to do. And, like many aircraft, the E-type has been stretched, because all models now feature the longer wheelbase of the earlier 2-plus-2 coupe version.

These comments apply to all Series 3 E-types which, in addition, now have anti-dive front suspension and, because of the increase in the wheelbase, more fore-and-aft interior room. But the model we are concerned with here is the one that goes bang twice as often — the V12/5.3-litre. Even if you don't read the V12 emblems, you can pick it out on the road by counting the four exhaust pipes as it overtakes you.

When the first E-type hit the headlines more than 10 years ago it had a 4.2 litre six-cylinder engine producing 265 bhp and a top speed nudging the 150 mph mark.

Now with the V12 we have a 5.3 litre engine producing 272 bhp . . . and a top speed nudging the 150 mph mark. Something has to be explained somewhere, as Hamlet remarked about the State of Denmark.

The performance of the original car was gradually whittled away by extra weight, poorer aerodynamics and a considerable drop in engine output to 171 bhp due to emission control equipment and an epidemic of frankness which ravaged the motor industry a few years ago.

E-type's ageing interior, poor switchgear layout. Though we tested a manual car, these shots were taken in an automatic we drove later.

However, note that the figures now quoted are net output whereas the original figure of 265 was gross. After all, many Americans buy E-types and you have to give them figures they can understand. It is certain that if a V12 unit were to be dropped into the original smooth body, the top speed would be very much higher — assuming the tyres would stand it for more than a mile. And there, in passing, is another reason for speed loss — fat tyres gobble up much more energy than skinny ones.

But perhaps in the present atmosphere of mass hysteria about so-called supercars it is a good thing to keep under 150 per. The actual figure is 148 and no doubt the missing 2 mph could be achieved by application of a good silicone polish. The car is still aerodynamically slippery, though, make no mistake about that, and if you suddenly press the clutch pedal or slip into neutral at high speed, it seems as though it will hurtle on and on forever and that the secret of perpetual motion isn't all that far from realisation. But the brakes are magnificent.

When you "knock it into neutral" it is very noticeable how quickly the revs drop and this is one of the characteristics of a V12, brought about by the extra friction and the lack of necessity for a big flywheel.

The result of this is that you need a fairly featherlight foot on the throttle if you are going to make immaculate gear changes during the getting-to-know-you session but after that it all comes quite naturally and anyone used to driving a Mazda Wankel will already have the technique. Perhaps it will be regarded as heretical to say that the engine is ideally suited to an automatic box.

The engine: hitherto, makers of V12s — modern ones, that is, and ignoring the efforts of such people as Lincoln — have gone in for high power at high revs with little in the basement.

Such a plan seems to me to be a complete waste of the engine type and Jaguar has very sensibly gone in for torque by the lorry load — 304 lb/ft at 3600 rpm is the actual figure. If you were to take one of the high-speed lifts out of the Empire State Building and lay it on its side you'd have some idea of the acceleration . . . though it still couldn't catch a Charger E49!

In actual figures, from a standing start you see 30 mph on the clock in 2.7 seconds, 60 in 6.4, 100 in 15.4 and at 120 you still have nearly 5 seconds change out of the half-minute.

V12 TYPE . . . A SWEETER SORT OF PURR

Mind you, the original 4.2 was half a second quicker to 120 but, up to 100, the V12 is well away. More significant, perhaps, are the top gear times from 20 to 40 (6.1 seconds) and 80 to 100 (6.4). In fact, any 20 mph step-up in speed, using top gear only, from 20 mph to 80, takes between 5.6 and 6.4 seconds, the best being 40-60 and 50-70 at 5.6, while 60-80 needs 5.7. Change down to third and you can knock roughly two seconds off these times up to the 90 mark.

But figures alone, impressive though they may be, don't reveal the outstandingly smooth manner of the V12's going. There is nothing else quite like it.

It is hardly necessary to change down from top at any time but the emphasis is on the word "necessary" because in practice, you frequently drop into third just for the sheer hell of the extra urge. On the road, the automatic reaction in most situations is to consider a quick change-down and acceleration in preference to using the brakes. Someone once described E-type acceleration as being like wet soap in the bath and the simile now applies even more. Or as Ronnie Corbett puts it: "No — that's me over there".

The clutch is on the heavy side though you can hardly blame it for this when you consider the amount of torque it has to transmit, but it is at a comfortable angle.

The change is firm and if not lightning quick, very positive. The ratios are obviously the result of a lot of thought and experimenting for it would be very difficult to find better ones to match the power unit. You can easily top 50 mph in first, 80 in second and 110 in third and the almost ridiculously low non-snatch speeds mean considerable overlapping of ratios for a given speed and, consequently, wide choice.

For example, at 30 mph you are driving quite sensibly whether you choose first, second, third or top, and similar situations apply at other speeds. Hence the car would be quite satisfactory with a torque coverter plus a dog clutch and no gears at all . . .

The engine isn't always an immediate starter from cold because it takes the mixture some time to get down the long pipes into the cylinders, but after a brief gefuffling period it settles down to a quiet tickover on half choke and warms up quickly. Up to 5000 rpm you can hardly hear it working and just under 7800 the valves tell you "No more!" The red line on the tacho is at 6500 rpm.

The thought of trying to balance four carburettors might be somewhat off-putting but with the right equipment there is no reason why it should be any more difficult than balancing two, but it wouldn't be a suck-it-and-see job.

One cannot help feeling that had Mercedes-Benz built this car it would have had petrol injection, but there is nothing as good as the Mercedes system available in Britain so Jag was probably wise to stick with carbs.

In any case, the lack of injection in part answers the often asked question: "How can Jaguar do it for the price?" The answer is: "You don't get anything for nothing" but, of course, it doesn't follow from that you always get value for money!

Fat tyres and revised suspension have produced greatly improved road-holding which means that "good" is now "even better". E-types have always been nicely balanced in the middle to produce over or understeer according to the dictates of your right foot and it doesn't take a lot of skill to change lanes on a bend by deliberately sliding the car bodily.

Continued on page11

SPECIFICATIONS AND PERFORMANCE DETAILS

MAKE . . . . **JAGUAR**
MODEL . . . . **E-TYPE SERIES 3 V12 COUPE**
BODY TYPE . . . . **COUPE**
PRICE **$11,293**

FUEL CONSUMPTION:
Overall . . . . 15 mpg
Cruising . . . . 15 mpg

SPEEDOMETER ERROR (mph):

Indicated	30	40	50	60	70	80	90
Actual	30	40	50	59	69	79	89

PERFORMANCE

MAXIMUM SPEEDS:
Fastest run . . . . 149 mph
Average of all runs . . . . 148 mph

IN GEARS:
1st . . . . 55 mph (6500 rpm)
2nd . . . . 83 mph (6500 rpm)
3rd . . . . 115 mph (6500 rpm)
4th . . . . 148 mph (6000 rpm)

ACCELERATION (through gears):
0-30 mph . . . . 2.7 secs
0-40 mph . . . . 3.4 secs
0-50 mph . . . . 4.6 secs
0-60 mph . . . . 6.4 secs
0-70 mph . . . . 7.9 secs
0-80 mph . . . . 9.8 secs
0-90 mph . . . . 12.6 secs
0-100 mph . . . . 15.4 secs
0-110 mph . . . . 19.3 secs
0-120 mph . . . . 25.8 secs

	3rd gear	4th gear
20-40 mph	4.2 secs	6.1 secs
30-50 mph	3.9 secs	6.0 secs
40-60 mph	3.7 secs	5.6 secs
50-70 mph	3.6 secs	5.6 secs

STANDING QUARTER MILE:
Fastest run . . . . 14.2 secs
Average of all runs . . . . 14.4 secs

BRAKING:
From 60 mph to 0 . . . . 133 ft

SPECIFICATIONS

ENGINE:
Cylinders V12
Bore and stroke . . . . (3.54 x 2.76 in.) 90 x 70 mm
Cubic capacity . . . . (326 cu in.) 5343 cc
Compression ratio . . . . 9 to 1
Valves . . . . Overhead with single camshafts
Carburettor . . . . Four Zenith 175CDSE
Power at rpm . . . . 272 bhp at 5850 rpm
Torque at rpm . . . . 304 lb/ft at 3600 rpm

TRANSMISSION:
Type . . . . Four-speed manual
Clutch . . . . 10.5 in. single plate

RATIO:

	direct	overall	mph per 1000 rpm
1st	2.933	9.00	10.1
2nd	1.905	5.85	12.8
3rd	1.389	4.26	18.7
4th	1.0	3.07	24.7
Final drive	3.07		

CHASSIS AND RUNNING GEAR:
Construction . . . . Unitary with front frame
Suspension front . . . . . Wishbones with torsion bars
Suspension rear . . . . Coil springs, single wishbones, swinging drive shafts, radius arms
Shock absorbers . . . . Telescopic
Steering type . . . . . Adwest assisted rack and pinion
Turns l to l 3.5
Turning circle . . . . 33.5 ft
Brakes type . . . . 4 Girling ventilated discs
Dimensions . . . . 11.2 in. front, 10.4 in. rear

DIMENSIONS:
Wheelbase . . . . 104.5 in. (265 cm)
Track front . . . . 54.5 in. (138 cm)
Track rear . . . . 53.0 in. (134 cm)
Length . . . . 15ft 4 in. (467 cm)
Width . . . . 6 ft 6¼ in. (160 cm)
Height . . . . 4 ft 1 in. (126 cm)
Fuel tank capacity . . . . 18 gal (81.8 litres)

TYRES:
Size E70VR-15
Pressures . . . . F28/R32 psi
Make on test car . . . . Dunlop SP Sport

END OF AN ERA

"A classic, my son, is that which endures by means of design and function . . . and which your generation, in all probability, will never produce."

Classics are made of more than mechanical components and certainly have more than functional value. If these alone were the criteria of a classic we would have to delete the overpowered and opulent beasts which inundate the classic car lists. Instead of mechanical innovations, we find that we must give a good deal of respect for age, allow for charisma, and finally throw in the fact that driving a classic makes the blood flow a bit faster through the veins.

That's what makes the Jaguar V-12 a classic. A short-lived three years in production has already seen the demise of the ultimate in the Jaguar roadster and coupe automobiles. Production lines halted on the E-type series last December, leaving a twelve-year echo in the E-Jaguar portion of the British Leyland shops. The V-12 version will no doubt become a contemporary classic.

The appeal of the Jaguar roadster has always been firmly based on the knowledge that Jaguar used the same suspension, engine, and braking components for the production line as was used on the racing cars.

Throughout the line of the XK-120, XK-140, XK-140 MC, XK-150 and the fabulous D-Type preceding theXK-SS and E-Type, there has been a direct link with the famous racing circuits of the world. It's amazing to find that Jaguar introduced their dual overhead cam six-cylinder in 1948, four-wheel disc brakes (inboard rear) in 1953, and a V-12 engine in 1971, all the while keeping the car's price far below the line of the "exotic" imports from Italy.

A prototype V-12 engine was first developed and tested in 1964–1966 when Jaguar had some thoughts about returning to international racing. This was a time when all the serious racing contestants were driving mid-engine cars, which probably influenced the Jaguar executives, a very front-thinking group, to give up the idea of competition. In a test of the new engine, however, a Jaguar was able to run laps of 161.5 mph at a test track.

With no competition plans in the hopper, the V-12 was tabled for lack of potential. It was too exotic for the road and too cumbersome for the track (Ferrari had already begun switching to V-8 engines.).

Jaguar engineers began taking a look at the V-12 from a reliability and road performance standpoint, contemplating a de-tuned version of the racing engine that might be considered versatile enough for everyday driving conditions. They had a vague idea for an introduction date in mind and raced against pricing structures, drooping profits, and emissions laws (U.S.) to adapt the engine for use in the E-Type and the XJ12 sedan.

The compression was dropped considerably, and flat-faced heads were used to provide a smoother acceleration pattern. The double-overhead cams were dropped in favor of the simpler single, and four Zenith-Strombergs replaced the fire-breathing six Webers of the racing engine. There was controversy between using an aluminum block or cast iron block, so Jaguar built one of each and found that the aluminum block had no appreciable noise difference and weighed 100 pounds less. The heads are aluminum alloy, as are other components, but rigidity and strength were the prime concern when engineers used seven main bearings with cast iron bearing caps and four securing bolts instead of two.

The end result was the current engine, coming off the production line with exotic performance and surprising reliability. The production line was the secret and allowed Jaguar to be the only manufacturer in the last 15–20 years to offer a V-12 engine in a car that sold for less than $10,000.

There are other reasons, though, that the E-Type V-12 will enter the classic field. The materials and workmanship put into the cars have not changed appreciably in spite of rising costs and increasing use of plastic and fiberglass components. We'd like to believe that, faced with the use of these compromises in the future, Jaguar declined and halted production.

Another such compromise with society was the addition of the ugly-looking but functional rubber bumpers mounted fore and aft to conform with the safety standards of the U.S. Jaguar undoubtedly saw a clean design being annually cluttered with tack-on features which would end the appeal of the car, V-12 engine or not.

Did we mention performance?

There's a little surge of excitement when you realize you're climbing into the cockpit of a real, honest-to-God V-12 machine, and we're no exception to the rule. The cockpit is neatly arrayed and instruments are scanned, aircraft style, as the luxurious leather seats soften the fall into the automobile . . . it's low!

The nice thing about tradition is that it makes you feel at home. Jaguar cockpits (that's the only word to describe them) have felt much the same way since 1950.

The starter motor begins with a low scream when the engine's cold. Just when you swear you've ruined something, the engine takes hold roughly because the manual choke is pulled all the way out. In normal temperatures the choke is only necessary in the extreme position for about five seconds. Then the second, or medium position will do nicely for warm-ups. The big engine warms surprisingly fast, and temperature reaches the normal range within a few blocks of moderate acceleration through the gears.

Ah, yes, the gears!

Jaguar engineers have always seemed to build transmissions for the heavy-handed, and the V-12 is no exception. The first reaction is to double-clutch because the gates require a "one-rest-two" sequence that totally discourages speed-shifting. It's smooth enough, but you just can't hurry a Jaguar box. On top of this, the clutch requires a lot of leg muscle. The big clutch must compensate for the tremendous torque of the V-12, but the two are in such harmonious linkage that the car will pull out very smoothly in first gear at an idle. The gear ratios are well-spaced for most driving conditions, but frustration sets in when you realize that 55 mph means third gear at 3400 rpm. What on earth do you do with the other 3000 rpm and the remaining fourth gear?

We were fortunate enough to run the test car on a closed track and experience the full potential of the V-12 powered car, though top speeds in third and fourth gears were not possible. Acceleration tests proved that the clutch was hefty enough for the V-12. If the clutch was dropped

at high revs the rear wheels spun viciously; if dropped at lower rpm's, the car would die on the line and slowly come back to life. The drivetrain, then, is really meant for everyday driving conditions in heavy traffic, slow running, and stop and go conditions that would tend to garbage up an exotic V-12 engine.

The V-12 is as docile as it is wild. It remains cool and even-running while idling through street traffic, without a hint of becoming cantankerous. The low compression ratio and smog-emissions tuning standards probably contribute to the even-temperedness of the otherwise explosive engine.

The smooth acceleration experienced in a V-12 is unparalleled and on a par with the new rotaries, though far more powerful. The V-12 Jaguar has power steering as standard equipment, which makes the beginning V-12 driver over-control as he strokes through the gears. The car is steering-sensitive anyway, and power steering makes it extremely touchy.

Power brakes on all four discs are also standard on the V-12, adding greatly to the overall handling characteristics while diving into chicanery. Just a touch here and a touch there on the pedal brings you into turns at exactly the desired speeds without nose-diving or rear-sliding.

The throttle response on the V-12 is so enthusiastic that down-shifting is no big problem. With a few hour's practice you can pick your gear and match it with a wide range of rpm to make a smooth selection. Up-shifting smoothly actually demands more practice and is definitely an acquired skill in the V-12.

The long hood with the raised proboscis conceals a myriad of metal which would scare off any filling-station mechanic. Until recent years Jaguar has suffered from a bad maintenance reputation due to the lack of a solid sales-service organization in the U.S. This has been resolved thoroughly, and Jaguar is fighting to keep owners from taking their cars to the local garage or lawnmower shop for service and repairs. There has been nothing wrong with the cars and engines that would justify a bad reputation, but their design and function is so different from U.S. engines that an entirely different frame of mind is necessary on the part of mechanics. In the case of the V-12, many people suggested it would be exactly twice the problems of the six-cylinder. It couldn't be further from the truth. This engine, so smooth and reliable, yet so wildly responsive to the throttle, will endure into the next decade with attentive maintenance. Though the V-12 roadster and coupe have been discontinued, the engine will still be manufactured for the XJ sedans for an indefinite period. The two best parts about owning a contemporary classic is having the last model of the production and, at the same time, knowing that you'll be able to find engine components.

We have a few nit-picking things to say about the V-12 roadster, so we may as well say them while the cars are still on the showroom floors. 1. Engine accessories require a gymnast mechanic or complete removal of the bonnet for servicing. 2. A battery condition meter is used instead of an ammeter, which is fine except that both could be used for more accurate electrical information. 3. The top, while folding into place very easily, will need to be removed for rear-window replacement almost annually if the owner lives in a climate where the top is up and down quite a lot. 4. Lastly, the very convenient feature of the remote-adjustable outside mirror on the driver's side is lost by the fact that the driver's knee most often knocks the mirror out of adjustment every time he enters or leaves the car.

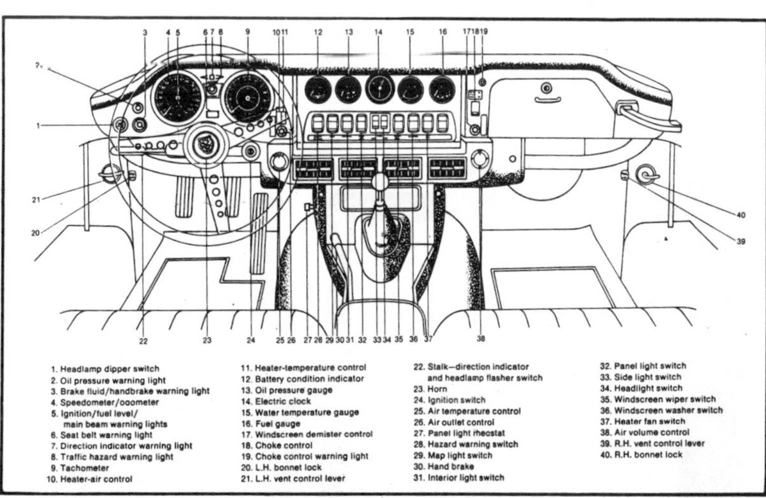

When the top is up the car offers a conversational environment. It is well insulated against the engine's noise, which is phenomenally quiet compared to other V-12s and rear-engined V-8s. The top flaps a bit on the frame, but not to the point of being annoying. With the air conditioning and stereo speaker system installed as standard equipment, the driver is allowed to create a very comfortable atmosphere regardless of touring speeds or traffic jams.

And it gets the looks.

Any kind of machine with a low-slung look, chrome wire wheels, and the almost jet-whine of a V-12 from the exhaust is going to get looks. While it may not be a prime concern to the V-12 owner, it is one of the mysterious qualities that can't be measured in mechanical and performance terms, but certainly relates to a classic. And most classics, sadly enough, relate to the end of an era.

JAGUAR E-TYPE V-12

PERFORMANCE DATA

Acceleration, sec:

0–30 mph	2.9
0–40 mph	4.1
0–50 mph	5.8
0–60 mph	7.4
0–70 mph	9.7
0–80 mph	12.4
Standing start, ¼ mile	16.39
Speed at end ¼ mile, mph	92.49
Avg accel over ¼ mile, g	0.257

Speeds in gears, mph:

1st (6500 rpm)	54
2nd (6500 rpm)	80
3rd (3400 rpm)	55
4th (2500 rpm)	65
Engine revs at 70 mph	3100

Speedometer error:

Electric speedometer	Car Speedometer
40 mph	39 mph
50 mph	49 mph
60 mph	59 mph
70 mph	69 mph
80 mph	78 mph

Brakes:

Min stopping distance from 60 mph, ft	146.5
Avg deceleration rate, g	0.821

Fuel economy:

Overall avg	9.2 mpg
Range on 21.7 gal tank	200 miles
Fuel required	premium

Skid pad:

Max speed on 100-ft rad, mph	32.95
Lateral acceleration, g	0.725

Interior noise, decibels (dBA):

Idle	60
Max 1st gear	64
Steady 40 mph	62
50 mph	66
60 mph	67
70 mph	70

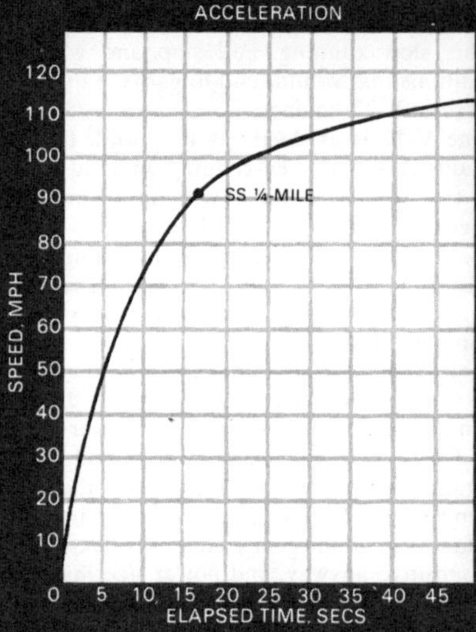

Graph Of Recorded Data Expressed In Percentage of 100 (100 = best possible rating)*

0 5 10 15 20 25 30 35 40 45 50 55 60 65 70 75 80 85 90 95 100

Acceleration
Brakes
Skid Pad
Interior Noise
Tire Reserve
Fuel Economy
Overall Rating
Best Car To Date (overall) — Jaguar E-Type V-12
Worst Car To Date (overall) — Mercedes 240D

SPECIFICATIONS

Engine:

Type	OHC V-12
Displacement, cu in	326
Displacement, cc	5343
Bore x stroke, in	3.54 x 2.76
Bore x stroke, mm	89.9 x 70.1
Compression ratio	7.8:1
Hp at rpm, net	241 at 5750
Torque at rpm, lb/ft, net	285 at 3500
Carburetion	4 1-V

Emissions, gm/mile:

Hydrocarbons	2.9
Carbon monoxide	37.0
Nitrogen oxides	2.9

Prices:

Factory list, as tested

West Coast	$9878
East Coast	$10,391

Accessories included in price: $160—wire wheels; $600—air conditioning; $240—am/fm stereo.

Manufacturer's guarantee and service:

Warranty (mos/miles)	12/12,000
Oil change (mos/miles)	—/6,000
Lubrication (mos/miles)	—/6,000
Tune-up (miles)	
Minor	6,000
Major	12,000

Driveline:

Transmission	4 spd manual
Gear ratios:	
1st	10.38:1
2nd	6.74:1
3rd	4.91:1
4th	3.54:1
Final drive ratio	3.31:1
Driving wheels	rear

Wheels and tires:

Wheels	6JK x 15
Tires	E70VR15
Reserve load, front/rear, lb	868/960

General:

Wheelbase, ins	105.0
Overall length, ins	189.6
Width, ins	66.06
Height, ins	48.4
Front track, ins	54.4
Rear track, ins	52.8
Trunk capacity, cu ft	4.75
Curb weight, lbs	3432
Distribution, % front/rear	53/47
Power-to-weight ratio, lbs/hp	14.24

Body and chassis:

Body/frame construction	unit/separate engine sub-frame
Brakes, front/rear	disc/disc
Swept area, sq in	442
Swept area, sq in/1000 lb	128.79
Steering	rack and pinion
Ratio	18:1
Turns, lock-to-lock	3.5
Turning circle, ft	36.0

Front suspension: Independent transverse wishbones, torsion bars, monotube hydraulic shock absorbers, and anti-roll bar; anti-dive geometry.

Rear suspension: wishbones with driveshaft forming upper link, radius arms, monotube hydraulic shock absorbers inside coil springs

Test Equipment Used: Testron Fifth Wheel, Esterline-Angus recorder, Ammco decelerometer, General Radio Sound Level Meter

* Acceleration (0-60 mph): 0% = 34.0 secs., 100% = 4.0 secs.; Brakes (60-0 mph): 0% = 220.0 ft., 100% = 140.0 ft.; Skid pad lateral accel.: 0% = 0.3 g, 100% = 0.9 g; Interior noise (70 mph): 0% = 90.0 dBA, 100% = 65.0 dBA; Tire reserve (with passengers): 0% = 0.0 lbs., 100% = 1500 lbs. or more; Fuel economy: 0% = 5 mpg, 100% = 45 mpg or more.

JAGUAR XK E

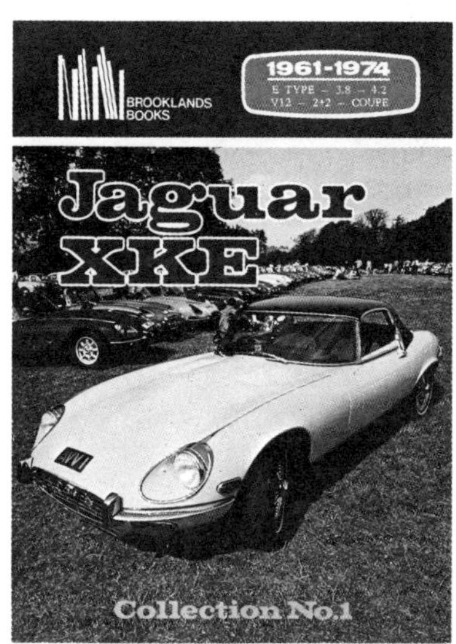

JAGUAR XKE
Collection No. 1

This collection of articles covers the whole production life of the XKE from 1961 to 1975, and supplements the Brooklands E-Type Marque Books with completely different articles. Five road tests are included, a comparison test against the Corvette and a 24 month report. They cover the 3.8, 4.2, V12, 2+2 and coupé models.
70 Large Pages.

Other articles on the XKE can be found in the following Brooklands titles: Jaguar Cars 1957-1961 (2), Jaguar Cars 1961-1964 (5), Jaguar Cars 1964-1968(3).

JAGUAR E TYPE 1961-1966

Road tests, new model introductions, technical descriptions, driving impressions, a report by Jack Brabham, a road research report and articles on touring, racing and supercharging make up this interesting book. Models covered are the 3.8, 4.2 roadsters and the 2+2 coupé.
100 Large Pages.

JAGUAR E TYPE 1966-1971

Articles in this book deal with road tests, the U.S. speed limit, a long term report, new model introductions, an XKE with a pontiac engine, Raymond Loweys XKE, U.S. Safety modifications, used car test of a 1964 fixed head E-type, comparison tests, technical reports and advice on buying a secondhand E-type. Models covered 4.2, 2+2, 2+2 automatic and V12.
100 Large Pages.

JAGUAR E TYPE 1971-1975

This book mainly deals with the Series III V12 model but reference is made to the Series I & II and the 1968 2+2. Road tests, comparison tests, new model introductions are all covered and articles on a 10,000 mile test, history, owner surveys, buying secondhand, touring and the New York Auto show are also included.
100 Large Pages.

These soft-bound volumes in the 'Brooklands Books' series consist of reprints of original road test reports and other articles that appeared in leading motoring journals during the periods concerned. Fully illustrated with photographs and cut-away drawings, the articles contain road impressions, performance figures, specifications, etc. None of the articles appears in more than one book. Sources include Autocar, Autosport, Car, Car & Driver, Cars & Car Conversions, Motor, Motor Racing, Modern Motor, Road Test, Road & Track and Wheels. Fascinating to read, the books are also invaluable as sources of historical reference and as practical aids to enthusiasts who wish to restore their cars to original condition.

From specialist booksellers or, in case of difficulty, direct from the distributors:
BROOKLANDS BOOK DISTRIBUTION, 'HOLMERISE', SEVEN HILLS ROAD, COBHAM, SURREY KT11 1ES, ENGLAND. Telephone: Cobham (09326) 5051
MOTORBOOKS INTERNATIONAL, OSCEOLA, WISCONSIN 54020, USA.
Telephone: 715 294 3345 & 800 826 6600

JAGUAR XJ SERIES

JAGUAR XJS 1975-1980

This book consists of 23 articles, 5 of which are Road Tests and 3 comparison tests Vs M-B 450 SLC, Lamborghini Espada III, Alfa Romeo Sprint & BMW 630 CSi & 528i. Also articles on touring and the XJ Spider.
100 Large Pages.

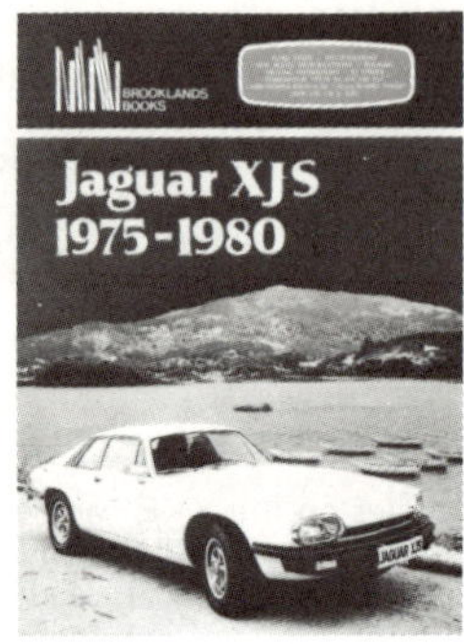

JAGUAR XJ12 1972-1980

A total of 9 road tests and thirteen other articles cover the V12 saloon story from its inception in 1972. Also included are owners reports comparison tests Vs M-B 500 SE and 450 SEL, Holden Caprice and FORD LTD. and tuning articles covering the coupé, XJ12L and the XJ5.3.
100 Large Pages.

JAGUAR XJ6 1968-1972

This is the first book in the XJ Series covers the early production years of this model. Seven road tests, a 10,000 and 18,000 mile report, a used car test, and owners reports on the 4.2 and 2.8 in all a total of 21 articles make up the story of the early XJ6.
100 Large Pages.

JAGUAR XJ6 1973-1980

This book continues the XJ6 story through the Series II & III models and covers the 3.4, 4.2, the XJ6L, the coupé and the Sedanca. A total of 8 road tests, plus articles on buying secondhand, touring, history and a 12,000 mile report. A total of 28 articles.
100 Large Pages.

These soft-bound volumes in the 'Brooklands Books' series consist of reprints of original road test reports and other articles that appeared in leading motoring journals during the periods concerned. Fully illustrated with photographs and cut-away drawings, the articles contain road impressions, performance figures, specifications, etc. None of the articles appears in more than one book. Sources include Autocar, Autosport, Car, Car & Driver, Cars & Car Conversions, Motor, Motor Racing, Modern Motor, Road Test, Road & Track and Wheels. Fascinating to read, the books are also invaluable as sources of historical reference and as practical aids to enthusiasts who wish to restore their cars to original condition.

From specialist booksellers or, in case of difficulty, direct from the distributors:
BROOKLANDS BOOK DISTRIBUTION, 'HOLMERISE', SEVEN HILLS ROAD, COBHAM, SURREY KT11 1ES, ENGLAND. Telephone: Cobham (09326) 5051
MOTORBOOKS INTERNATIONAL, OSCEOLA, WISCONSIN 54020, USA.
Telephone: 715 294 3345 & 800 826 6600